Boulder City Town Company Lot Sales

1859–1864

An Annotated Map Guide

Compiled by Dina C. Carson

Boulder City
Town Company
Lot Sales 1859-1864

An Annotated Map Guide

Compiled by Dina C. Carson

Published by:

Iron Gate Publishing
P.O. Box 999
Niwot, CO 80544
www.irongate.com

Copyright © 2015 by Dina C. Carson, Iron Gate Publishing

Printed in the United States of America

ISBN   1-879579-87-1   ISBN 13   978-1-879579-87-3

Introduction

The original records for the Boulder City Town Company are held in the archives of the University of Colorado. There are copies available at the Carnegie Branch Library for Local History in Boulder, Colorado.

The original records consist of one journal that contains a set of Constitution and By Laws for the town, the minutes of the Boulder City Town Company, the land lottery sales showing each "interest" and the lots assigned to that shareholder, as well as a section showing the transfers of property by lots.

The other journal records the sale or transfer of property including horses, cows, saw mills, saw mill equipment, houses and lots.

During the initial meeting of the Boulder City Town Company a committee was formed to hire a surveyor. An initial survey was conducted with the final survey conducted by J M Schaeffer in July of 1859. Boulder City was not laid out in strict east-west, north-south grid. Its main street, Pearl Street, was laid out to run from the foothills to Valmont Butte, some five miles to the east.

This book takes the individual transactions from both journals and arranges them by date in an effort to see who was in Boulder city when, and what activity was taking place.

Because no original survey map of Boulder City exists, I took the plat map of 1864 that does not include street names, along with maps from 1868 (a partial view of downtown), 1871 and 1887 that showed the old block numbers and created a map of what the original survey could have looked like using the same numbering method as the later maps. The blocks and block numbers are almost exactly the same. The two exceptions are an unnumbered block where the courthouse stands currently (between 13th and 14th Streets, and Pearl and Spruce Streets), and an unnumbered block between 16th and 17th Streets, and Hill [now Mapleton] and Bluff Streets. I believe these two lots were intended to be left unnumbered and used as public squares—one for the courthouse, the other for a school, perhaps.

The blocks were laid out in 12 lot blocks with lots 1–6 on the north side, and lots 7–12 on the south. The lots are numbered consecutively from east to west along the north edge of the block, and then from west to east along the southern edge. Along 20th Street there is an anomaly. The blocks just west of 20th Street have only 10 lots and the blocks east of 20th Street have 14. My best guess is that there was already a road running through the area along what would become 20th Street, and rather than moving the road, the surveyor altered the size of the blocks to accommodate the road.

There were 60 original interest holders in Boulder City, each with four shares. Each share entitled the holder to eighteen lots in Boulder City, Boulder Valley, Nebraska. These interests were assigned on 10 Feb 1859. By the time of the first land lottery, however, many interests had already changed owners.

On 11 Aug 1859, the first share of each interest was assigned lots by lottery. I created a second map showing the results of the land auction on 11 Aug 1859. The great majority of lots were taken between 3rd and 17th Streets, Water and Bluff Streets—essentially greater downtown.

On 20 September 1859, the certificates of stock were issued, showing even more transfers of interests and shares, resulting in a third map showing those landholders.

Some street names have changed, including:
- Hill Street is now Mapleton Avenue
- Front Street is now Walnut Street
- Water Street is now Canyon Boulevard

What follows are the sales of property as they are recorded in the Boulder City Town Company Journals, in order of date, along with a small map of the block. The second half of the book shows each block in order from block 1–200. When full shares are sold, you will need to consult the illustrations in the back of the book. Space did not permit showing illustrations for sales of full shares.

The maps are available through Iron Gate Publishing on plain paper or on velum for library use, at www.irongate.com.

1859

25 Feb 1859, James P McChesney to Theodore Squires, Interest No. 41

3 Mar 1859, John McKay to Isaac S Bull [Buell], Interest No. 38

9 Mar 1859, one entire original interest donated to Jno D Henderson

12 Mar 1859, Isaac S Bull [Buell] to John L Buell, Interest No 38

14 Mar 1859, D M Wooley to A A Brookfield, 1/2 interest No. 57 including 1/2 house on lot 12 block 120

14 Mar 1859, J P Brown to D M Woolley, 1/2 interest No. 7 including 1/2 of house on Lot no 2 in B[lock] 68

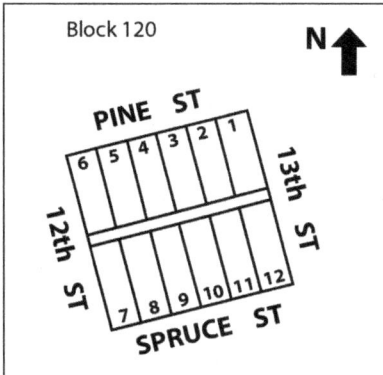

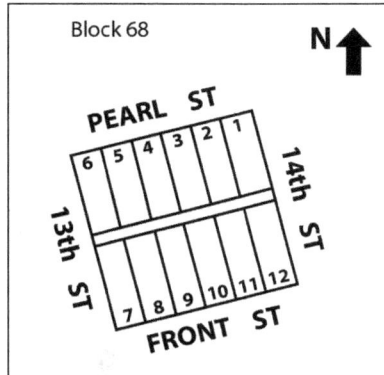

31 Mar 1859, A E Baugh to Daniel Blocher, four lots of Interest No. 8

18 Apr 1859, Dennison J Ely to Franklin Winslow, Interest No. 26

25 Apr 1859, John Moran to D S Corbin, Interest No. 43

26 Apr 1859, J P Fray to C M Clouser, Interest No. 50 including house (no lot or block no)

26 April 1859, Alfred Miller to Bicknell, Cook, Hotchkiss & Buckwalter, Interest No. 39 including house on lot 12 block 122

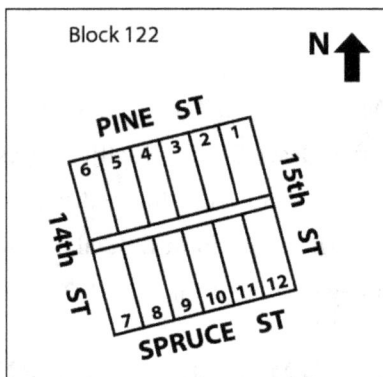

28 Apr 1859, Thomas Lorton to A A Brookfield, Interest No. 37 including house (no block and lot no)

29 Apr 1859, John Cassity to M D Cowsert, Interest No. 22

29 Mar 1859, Daniel Blocher to B A Sinn, lot 4 block 66; lot 7 block 66; lot 7 block 99

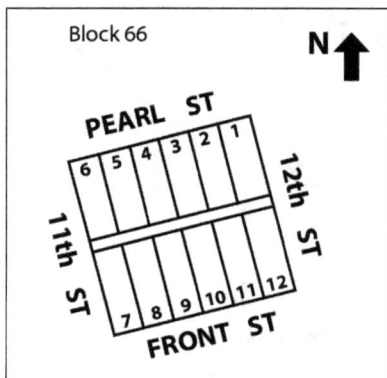

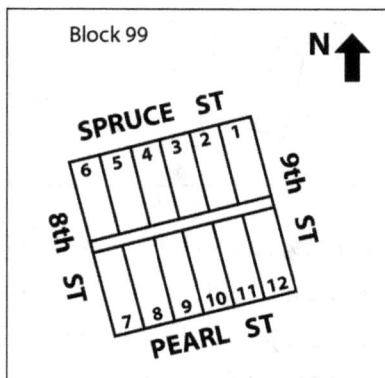

30 Apr 1859, A A Brookfield to George Dixon, 1/2 Interest No. 37

2 May 1859, George Briggs to G R Williamson, 1/2 Interest No. 9 including 1/2 house (no block or lot no)

2 May 1859, George Hackleman to M W Towner, Interest No. 31 including house (no block or lot no)

6 May 1859, John E Williams to Daniel Blocher, Interest No. 52 including house on lot 8, block 121

18 June 1859, Silas D Burns to A M Bookham, Interest No. 12, including the house on lot 1, block 67

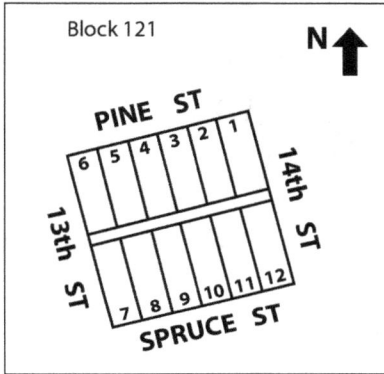

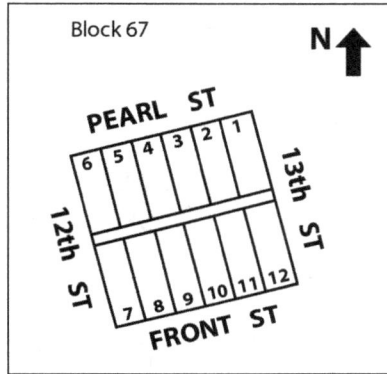

20 June 1859, J P Brown to Thorp & Winslow, 1/2 interest no. 7 to G W Thorp and Franklin Winslow including 1/2 house and lot no 2, block 68 (See earlier transaction to D M Wooley on 14 Mar 1859)

28 June 1859, S D Hotchkiss to M D Cowsert, Interest No. 28 including house on Lot 1, block 95

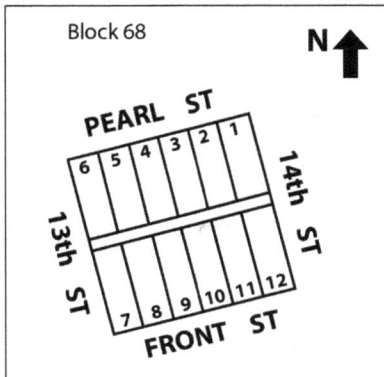

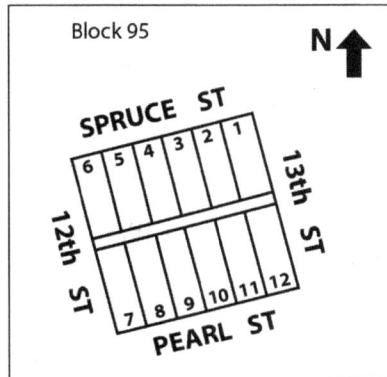

2 July 1859, Tarbox & Donnelly donated lots 11 & 12, Block 97

2 July 1859, lots 1-10, block 97 donated for the erection of a Saw mill on Boulder Creek

2 July 1859, lot 11, block 94 to Clark W Heath to build a building 17x25, 1.5 stories high

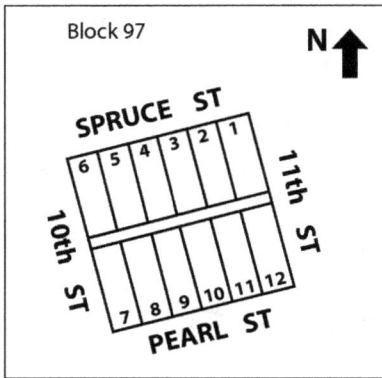

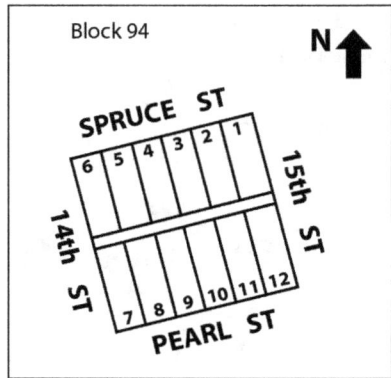

2 July 1859, lot 6, block 65; lot 2, block 42 to Wm M Barney to erect a building 2 stories high

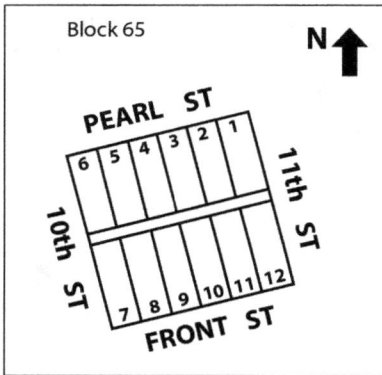

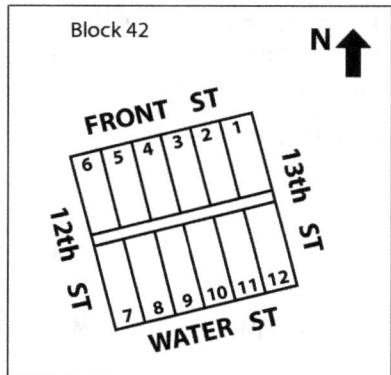

2 July 1859, donated lot 10, block 120 to J H Greenly to build a building 16x24, 1.5 stories high

Block 120

PINE ST
6 5 4 3 2 1
12th ST
13th ST
7 8 9 10 11 12
SPRUCE ST

N

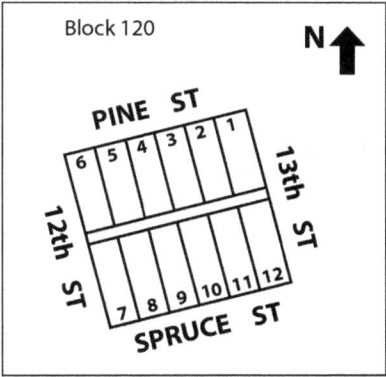

3 July 1859, John R Hall to T J Jones, house (no block or lot no)

14 July 1859, George Dixon to C W Sears, George Chapman, A E Baugh & T R Hamilton, 1/4 Interest No. 25

22 July 1859, M D Cowsert to Edward Donnelly, 2 lots (lot and block no not recorded)

25 July 1859, Charles M Clouser to Thorp & Winslow, 1/2 of Interest No. 50 including 1/2 house (no lot or block no)

25 July 1859, Albert Corbin has transferred Interest No. 18, including the house on lot 6, block 95 to John W Stokes

27 July 1859, D M Wooley to Thorp & Winslow, 1/2 house on lot 2, block 68 to G W Thorp and Franklin Winslow

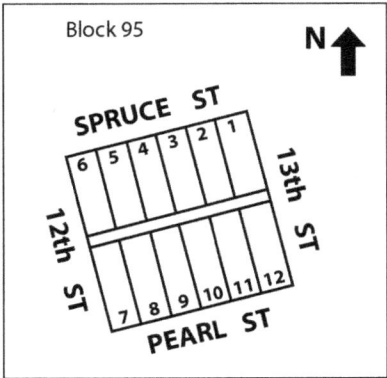

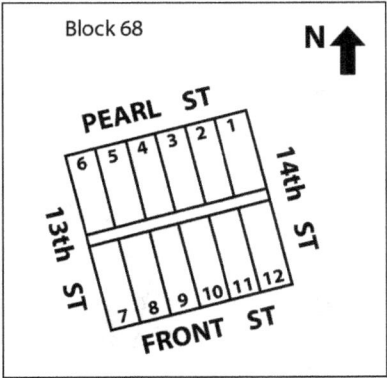

Block 95

SPRUCE ST
6 5 4 3 2 1
12th ST
13th ST
7 8 9 10 11 12
PEARL ST

N

Block 68

PEARL ST
6 5 4 3 2 1
13th ST
14th ST
7 8 9 10 11 12
FRONT ST

N

28 July 1859, David M Woolley to David King & Bros, 1/2 interest No. 7

30 July 1859, Louis C Davenport by his agent D M Woolley, to Wm Vandiver, 1/2 Interest No. 24

30 July 1859, M D Cowsert to Goss, Pell and Lowe, Interests No. 22 and 28

30 July 1859, John L Buell to Goss, Pell & Lowe, Interest No. 5, including the house built on lot no 11, block 95 (C J Goss, W G Pell, R S Lowe)

1 Aug 1859, David Horsfall to Alvah Fay, the house on lot 12 block 67

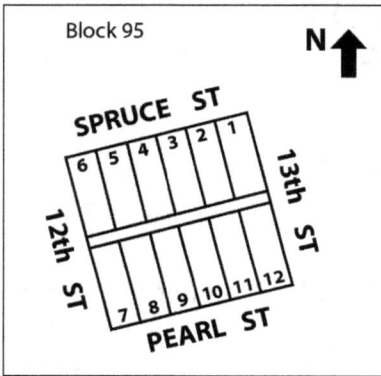

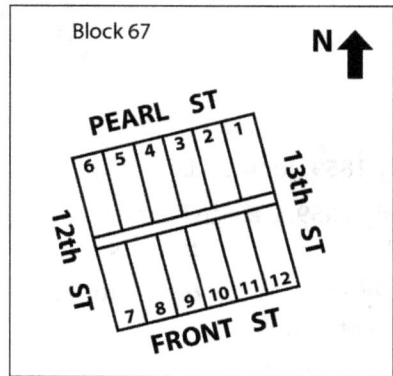

2 Aug 1859, A B Perrington to Franklin Mayze [Mays], house on lot 12 block 121

2 Aug 1859, Louis C Davenport by his agent D M Woolley, to A Barker, 1/2 Interest No. 24, including the house on lot 4 block 95

2 August 1859, Isaac S Buell to P G Cooper, Interest No. 4, including the house on lot 9, block 95

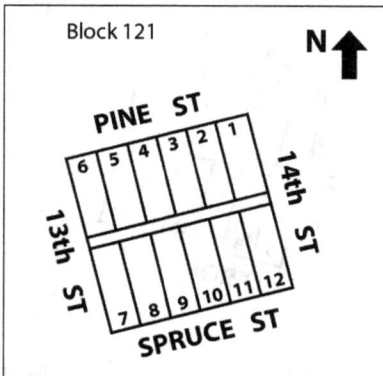

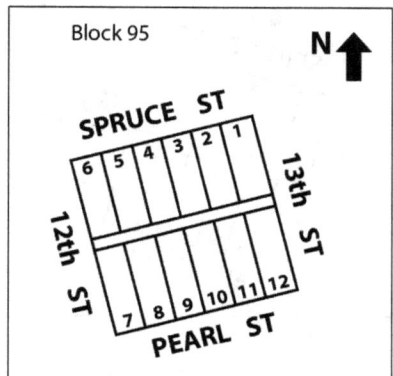

4 Aug 1859, M W Towner to Theodore Squires, 1/4 Interest No. 31

4 Aug 1859, Theodore Squires to M W Towner, Interest No. 49, including house (no lot or block no)

8 Aug 1859, G R Williamson to Wm M Barney, 1/2 interest No. 9 including 1/2 house and lot no 6, block 67

10 Aug 1859, donation to J H Greenly, lot 10 block 120

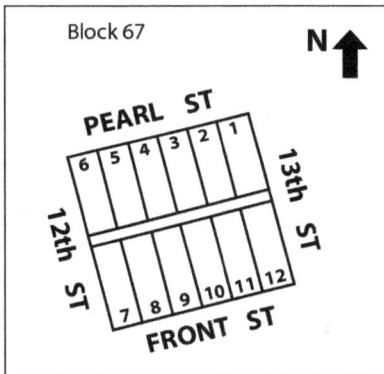

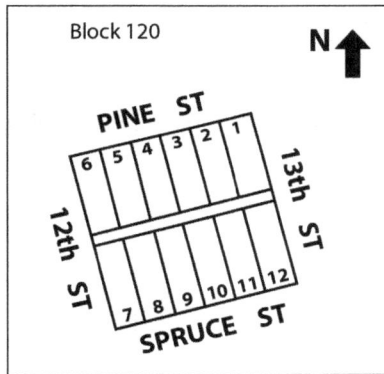

10 Aug 1859, donation to J P B Irwin, lot 2 block 65

10 Aug 1859, donation to Clark W Heath, S E Strorson (Steoeson), Charles Davis, J F Davis, I W Davis, W P Butler, G F Pharo, H H Stowe, Rufus Trowbridge, Chas Gardner, Freeman Belcher, and J B Kinsley, lot 1 block 96

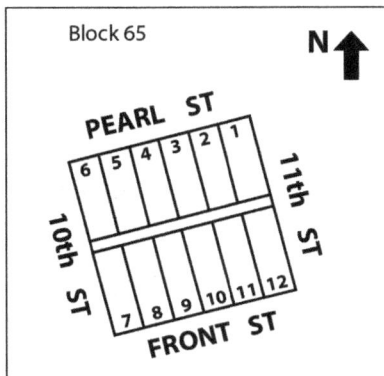

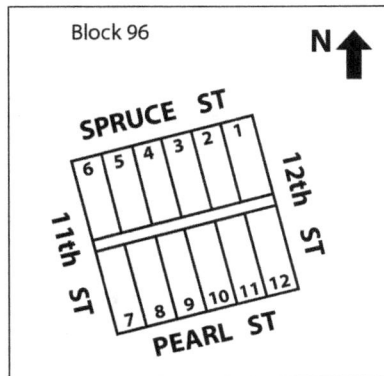

LAND AUCTION

On 11 Aug 1859 the official land auction was held. It wasn't until September 20th, 1859 that the interest certificates were issued. Some interests changed hands in the month and a half between those dates. The lots are shown in the order they were drawn, from left to right. [See individual blocks starting on page 91].

Interest No. 1

11 Aug 1859, James Able [Abel] lots drawn (block 8, lot 5 was on the list on September 20th, block 112, lot 2 was not), block 67 lot 2 was sold to D Pound

block	lot	block	lot	block	lot	block	lot
118	8	64	12	43	3	121	6
59	4	41	9	115	6	112	2
111	3	46	7	112	2	58	10
153	1	178	11	174	10	146	10
178	3	67	2	[8]	[5]		

20 Sept 1859, Boulder City Town Company to Daniel Williams, Interest No. 1, Share No. 1
20 Sept 1859, Boulder City Town Company to Daniel Williams, Interest No. 1, Share No. 2
20 Sept 1859, Boulder City Town Company to Daniel Williams, Interest No. 1, Share No. 3
20 Sept 1859, Boulder City Town Company to Daniel Williams, Interest No. 1, Share No. 4

Interest No. 2

11 Aug 1859, Thomas A Akins [Akins] lots drawn; **20 Sept 1859**, interest no. 2 transferred from Thomas Akins to Edward Donelly, **7 Nov 1859**, interest no. 2 transferred back to Thomas Akins except block 64, lot 3 and block 44, lot 6 which were kept by E Donnelly

block	lot	block	lot	block	lot	block	lot
119	11	64	3	44	6	60	6
115	11	111	12	115	5	152	11
46	10	123	4	148	6	147	5

block	lot	block	lot	block	lot	block	lot
10	7	145	8	68	4	121	5
113	6	172	9				

20 Sept 1859, Boulder City Town Company to Edward Donnelly, Interest No.2, Share No. 1
20 Sept 1859, Boulder City Town Company to Edward Donnelly, Interest No.2, Share No. 2
20 Sept 1859, Boulder City Town Company to Edward Donnelly, Interest No.2, Share No. 3
20 Sept 1859, Boulder City Town Company to Edward Donnelly, Interest No.2, Share No. 4

Interest No. 3

11 Aug 1859, Charles B Aikins [Akins] lots drawn; **20 Sept 1859** block 64, lot 4; block 112, lot 12; and block 115, lot 10 went to J Roberson & Co. The remaining lots were conveyed to H C Norton & M B Boughton on **5 Nov 1859**.

block	lot	block	lot	block	lot	block	lot
119	10	64	4	44	1	60	7
112	12	114	2	151	8	13	7
115	10	149	1	146	5	172	10
123	3	175	3	121	4	46	11
10	12(only 17 lots recorded)						

20 Sept 1859, Boulder City Town Company to Charles B Akins, Interest No.3, Share No. 1
20 Sept 1859, Boulder City Town Company to Charles B Akins, Interest No.3, Share No. 2
20 Sept 1859, Boulder City Town Company to Charles B Akins, Interest No.3, Share No. 3
20 Sept 1859, Boulder City Town Company to Charles B Akins, Interest No.3, Share No. 4

Interest No. 4

11 Aug 1859, Isaac S Buell lots drawn transferred to P G Cooper, house already on block 95 lot 9

block	lot	block	lot	block	lot	block	lot
65	4	100	6	51	12	99	3
112	8	50	5	40	1	158	8
169	10	61	7	71	12	165	1
118	5	14	10	170	4	103	9
71	10	95	9				

20 Sept 1859, Boulder City Town Company to P G Cooper, Interest No. 4, Share No. 1
20 Sept 1859, Boulder City Town Company to P G Cooper, Interest No. 4, Share No. 2
20 Sept 1859, Boulder City Town Company to P G Cooper, Interest No. 4, Share No. 3
20 Sept 1859, Boulder City Town Company to P G Cooper, Interest No. 4, Share No. 4

Interest No. 5

11 Aug 1859, Jno [John] L Buell lots drawn transferred to C J Goss, Pell & Lowe, except block 95, lot 11 to Daniel Pound, block 116 lot 12 and block 100, lot 3 to E C Thompson

block	lot	block	lot	block	lot	block	lot
94	3	111	1	147	2	116	12
115	2	176	11	45	4	17	7
9	12	61	1	45	11	145	11
119	4	124	10	152	8	100	3
147	1	95	11				

20 Sept 1859, Boulder City Town Company to C J Goss, W G Pell and R S Lowe, Interest No. 5, Share No. 1
20 Sept 1859, Boulder City Town Company to C J Goss, W G Pell and R S Lowe, Interest No. 5, Share No. 2
20 Sept 1859, Boulder City Town Company to C J Goss, W G Pell and R S Lowe, Interest No. 5, Share No. 3
20 Sept 1859, Boulder City Town Company to C J Goss, W G Pell and R S Lowe, Interest No. 5, Share No. 4

Interest No. 6

11 Aug 1859, W S Buckwalter lots drawn transferred to David Stone & Co (block 69, lot 2 (listed on the 20 Sept, not listed 11 Augt)

block	lot	block	lot	block	lot	block	lot
118	10	115	12	152	1	64	10
113	4	145	3	43	5	111	5
174	8	60	6	45	7	146	8
120	2	12	4	178	5	43	8
58	8	69	2				

20 Sept 1859, Boulder City Town Company to W S Buckwalter, Interest No. 6, Share No. 1
20 Sept 1859, Boulder City Town Company to W S Buckwalter, Interest No. 6, Share No. 2
20 Sept 1859, Boulder City Town Company to W S Buckwalter, Interest No. 6, Share No. 3

20 Sept 1859, Boulder City Town Company to W S Buckwalter, Interest No. 6, Share No. 4 (block 60, lot 6—also listed to Edward Donnelly; block 118, lot 10—also listed to Albert Corbin)

Interest No. 7

11 Aug 1859, J [John] P Brown lots drawn transferred to H S Buckwalter (crossed out), 1/2 to D M Woolley, 1/2 to Thorp & Winslow; 1/2 from D M Wooley to David King & Bro; block 68 lot 2 specifically to Thorp & Winslow

block	lot	block	lot	block	lot	block	lot
65	7	101	7	4	7	99	4
111	9	51	3	70	10	158	3
68	10	61	11	71	6	167	6
150	12	15	5	169	5	104	10
17	8	68	2				

20 Sept 1859, Boulder City Town Company to George W Thorp & Frank Winslow, Interest No. 7, Share No. 1

20 Sept 1859, Boulder City Town Company to George W Thorp & Frank Winslow, Interest No. 7, Share No. 2

20 Sept 1859, Boulder City Town Company to George W Thorp & Frank Winslow, Interest No. 7, Share No. 3

20 Sept 1859, Boulder City Town Company to George W Thorp & Frank Winslow, Interest No. 7, Share No. 4

20 Sept 1859, David King & Bros to Thorp & Winslow, 1/2 Interest No. 7 [the following lots:]

block	lot	block	lot	block	lot	block	lot
65	7	4	7	99	4	111	9
51	3	70	10	150	12	15	5
169	3	104	10				

20 Sept 1859, Thorp & Winslow to David King & Bros, the following lots:

block	lot	block	lot	block	lot	block	lot
61	11	101	7	158	3	71	6
17	8	68	10	167	6		

Interest No. 8

11 Aug 1859, Albert E Baugh lots drawn, 4 lots transferred to Daniel Blocher—block 118, lot 11; block 64, lot 7; block 59, lot 1; block 114, lot 12

block	Lot	block	lot	block	lot	block	lot
118	11	64	7	44	5	59	1
120	3	43	9	114	12	113	3
112	4	45	12	12	5	47	5
151	6	145	4	173	11	12	7
176	2	(only 17 lots recorded)					

20 Sept 1859, Boulder City Town Company to Albert E Baugh, Interest No. 8, Share No. 1
20 Sept 1859, Boulder City Town Company to A E Baugh, Interest No. 8, Share No. 2
20 Sept 1859, Boulder City Town Company to A E Baugh, Interest No. 8, Share No. 3
20 Sept 1859, Boulder City Town Company to A E Baugh, Interest No. 8, Share No. 4

Interest No. 9

11 Aug 1859, George [W] Briggs lots drawn transferred 1/2 to George Williamson, 1/2 from Williamson to Wm Barney; lots to Wm Barney block 67, lot 6; block 67, lot 9; block 98, lot 7; block 150, lot 11; block 154, lot 1; block 103, lot 3; block 147, lot 8; block 49, lot 9; block 171, lot 6

block	lot	block	lot	block	lot	block	lot
67	9	154	1	176	7	98	7
103	3	49	9	93	9	156	3
167	8	62	6	38	6	171	6
150	10	147	8	167	5	150	11
39	10	67	6				

20 Sept 1859, George Briggs to Wm M Barney, 1/2 Interest No. 9[, including the following lots:]

block	lot	block	lot	block	lot	block	lot
176	7	93	9	156	3	167	8
62	8	38	6	150	10	167	5
30	10						

20 Sept 1859, Wm M Barney to George Briggs, Interest No. 9, 1/2 share No. 4 and share No. 2, along with the following lots:

block	lot	block	lot	block	lot	block	lot
67	9	98	7	49	9	147	8
67	6	154	1	103	3	171	6
150	11						

20 Sept 1859, Boulder City Town Company to William M Barney, Interest No. 9, Share No. 1
20 Sept 1859, Boulder City Town Company to William M Barney, Interest No. 9, Share No. 2
20 Sept 1859, Boulder City Town Company to William M Barney, Interest No. 9, Share No. 3
20 Sept 1859, Boulder City Town Company to William M Barney, Interest No. 9, Share No. 4

Interest No. 10

11 Aug 1859, Daniel Blocher lots drawn, transferred block 66, lot 4 to B A Sinn, H L Tracy; block 99, lot 7, to B A Sinn, Jno L Buell; Block 101, lot 1, to A C M Brian [A C McBrian]

block	lot	block	lot	block	lot	block	lot
66	4	99	7	70	5	61	9
151	12	104	8	101	1	104	5
157	5	39	1	15	3	17	10
5	7	50	11	168	8	168	6
169	3			(only 17 lots listed)			

20 Sept 1859, Boulder City Town Company to Daniel Blocher, Interest No. 10, Share No. 1
20 Sept 1859, Boulder City Town Company to Daniel Blocher, Interest No. 10, Share No. 2
20 Sept 1859, Boulder City Town Company to Daniel Blocher, Interest No. 10, Share No. 3
20 Sept 1859, Boulder City Town Company to Daniel Blocher, Interest No. 10, Share No. 4

Interest No. 11

11 Aug 1859, Albert G Baber, lots drawn donated to J D Henderson, and sold to W G Pell for taxes

block	lot	block	lot	block	lot	block	lot
119	7	64	8	44	3	59	12
120	5	43	11	113	12	114	5
151	11	12	6	46	4	47	3

block	lot	block	lot	block	lot	block	lot
150	6	146	2	173	9	11	7
176	4			(only 17 lots listed)			

20 Sept 1859, Boulder City Town Company to Albert Baber, Interest No. 11, Share No. 1
20 Sept 1859, Boulder City Town Company to Albert Baber, Interest No. 11, Share No. 2
20 Sept 1859, Boulder City Town Company to Albert Baber, Interest No. 11, Share No. 3
20 Sept 1859, Boulder City Town Company to Albert Baber, Interest No. 11, Share No. 4

Interest No. 12

11 Aug 1859, Silas D Burns lots drawn transferred to A M Bookham, from Bookham to W S & W B Edson; block 67, lot 1 marked for A M Bookham (not listed below and block 124, lot 3 listed on the September list is probably block 174 lot 3)

block	lot	block	lot	block	lot	block	lot
23	7	113	1	47	6	116	9
116	2	148	2	42	3	153	8
175	11	60	2	145	1	7	7
120	6	44	11	174	3	42	9
124	3	[67]	[1]	(only 17 lots listed)			

20 Sept 1859, Boulder City Town Company to T J Jones, Interest No. 12, Share No. 1
20 Sept 1859, Boulder City Town Company to T J Jones, Interest No. 12, Share No. 2
20 Sept 1859, Boulder City Town Company to T J Jones, Interest No. 12, Share No. 3
20 Sept 1859, Boulder City Town Company to T J Jones, Interest No. 12, Share No. 4

Interest No. 13

11 Aug 1859, A A Brookfield lots drawn (no lots listed on 20 Sept, all listed on 11 Aug); block 95, lot 3 transferred to D Pound; block 66, lot 10 transferred to Wm M Skinner

block	lot	block	lot	block	lot	block	lot
95	3	68	10	66	10	93	4
62	7	104	1	148	8	157	7
101	5	153	5	14	6	38	3
16	11	172	7	48	8	165	10
174	6	166	2				

20 Sept 1859, Boulder City Town Company to A A Brookfield, Interest No. 13, Share No. 1
20 Sept 1859, Boulder City Town Company to A A Brookfield, Interest No. 13, Share No. 2
20 Sept 1859, Boulder City Town Company to A A Brookfield, Interest No. 13, Share No. 3
20 Sept 1859, Boulder City Town Company to A A Brookfield, Interest No. 13, Share No. 4
(block 68, lot 10 already listed to David King & Bro)

Interest No. 14

11 Aug 1859, David S Corbin lots drawn, forfeited to the company, 10 Sept 1859 sold for taxes to T J Jones; block 94, lot 9 (not listed below) also had a house (built by David S Corbin); block 68, lot 11 to Wm Parks (crossed out for T J Jones); block 66, lot 9 to Wm Parks (crossed out for T J Jones); block 63, lot 12 to Wm Parks (crossed out for T J Jones); block 148, lot 9 to D P [probably Daniel Pound]; block 157, lot 1 to D P; block 153, lot 4 to D P

block	lot	block	lot	block	lot	block	lot
68	11	66	9	93	3	63	12
104	6	148	9	157	1	101	4
153	4	14	12	38	2	16	10
171	12	48	9	165	9	174	1
51	7	[94]	[9]				

20 Sept 1859, Boulder City Town Company to David S Corbin, Interest No. 14, Share No. 1
20 Sept 1859, Boulder City Town Company to David S Corbin, Interest No. 14, Share No. 2
20 Sept 1859, Boulder City Town Company to David S Corbin, Interest No. 14, Share No. 3
20 Sept 1859, Boulder City Town Company to David S Corbin, Interest No. 14, Share No. 4
(block 68, lot 11, block 66, lot 9, block 63, lot 12, block 101, lot 4 already listed as transferred
  to David S Corbin)

Interest No. 15

11 Aug 1859, George Bicknel [Bicknell] lots drawn, sold for taxes to T J Jones & Redener (no lots recorded on 20 Sept, all listed on 11 Aug)

block	lot	block	lot	block	lot	block	lot
65	5	99	1	40	3	60	10
148	12	103	11	44	7	110	10
158	10	92	7	14	2	71	5
50	7	51	4	169	8	165	7
171	2	(only 17 lots recorded)					

20 Sept 1859, Boulder City Town Company to UNRECORDED, Interest No. 15, Share No. 1
20 Sept 1859, Boulder City Town Company to UNRECORDED, Interest No. 15, Share No. 2
20 Sept 1859, Boulder City Town Company to UNRECORDED, Interest No. 15, Share No. 3
20 Sept 1859, Boulder City Town Company to UNRECORDED, Interest No. 15, Share No. 4

Interest No. 16

11 Aug 1859, H W Childs [Chiles] lots drawn (no lots recorded on 20 Sept, all recorded on 11 Aug)

block	lot	block	lot	block	lot	block	lot
69	8	65	11	93	1	63	11
104	12	148	11	156	1	101	2
153	2	15	7	38	10	16	8
170	12	48	11	165	5	175	1
51	9		(only 17 lots recorded)				

20 Sept 1859, Boulder City Town Company to H W Childs (Chiles), Intst No. 16, Share No. 1
20 Sept 1859, Boulder City Town Company to H W Childs (Chiles), Intst No. 16, Share No. 2
20 Sept 1859, Boulder City Town Company to H W Childs (Chiles), Intst No. 16, Share No. 3
20 Sept 1859, Boulder City Town Company to H W Childs (Chiles), Intst No. 16, Share No. 4

Interest No. 17

11 Aug 1859, Charles E Cook lots drawn, sold for taxes to Jno [John] L Buell & E Donnelly (no lots listed on 20 Sept, all listed on 11 Aug)

block	lot	block	lot	block	lot	block	lot
96	3	117	11	42	6	59	10
117	6	101	11	41	7	114	9
156	10	123	1	13	2	92	5
48	7	150	3	171	9	5	1
173	2		(only 17 lots listed)				

20 Sept 1859, Boulder City Town Company to C E Cook, Interest No. 17, Share No. 1
20 Sept 1859, Boulder City Town Company to C E Cook, Interest No. 17, Share No. 2
20 Sept 1859, Boulder City Town Company to C E Cook, Interest No. 17, Share No. 3
20 Sept 1859, Boulder City Town Company to C E Cook, Interest No. 17, Share No. 4

Interest No. 18

11 Aug 1859, Albert Corbin lots drawn, transferred to John W Stokes, transferred from John W Stokes to Robinson & Tracy; block 95, lot 6 has a house

block	lot	block	lot	block	lot	block	lot
67	11	98	9	93	10	62	12
58	6	149	9	154	6	102	5
154	5	16	1	147	10	39	2
174	7	49	5	166	10	172	6
167	3	95	6				

20 Sept 1859, Boulder Town Co. to James Robinson & Hartwell S Tracy, Interest No. 18, Share No. 1
20 Sept 1859, Boulder Town Co. to James Robinson & Hartwell S Tracy, Interest No. 18, Share No. 2
20 Sept 1859, Boulder Town Co. to James Robinson & Hartwell S Tracy, Interest No. 18, Share No. 3
20 Sept 1859, Boulder Town Co. to James Robinson & Hartwell S Tracy, Interest No. 18, Share No. 4
(Block 174, lot 7 already listed to W S and W B Edson, the house on block 95, lot 6 is already listed to John W Stokes)

Interest No. 19

11 Aug 1859, Nicholas Connelly lots drawn; block 9, lot 12 with house to S W Tower (not listed on the 20 Sept list)

block	lot	block	lot	block	lot	block	lot
96	6	63	2	41	2	61	2
122	6	101	8	42	12	113	11
157	11	124	6	13	10	92	9
49	6	151	2	170	8	167	12
172	3	[9]	[12]				

20 Sept 1859, Boulder City Town Company to Nicholas Connelly Intst No. 19, Share No. 1
20 Sept 1859, Boulder City Town Company to Nicholas Connelly Intst No. 19, Share No. 2
20 Sept 1859, Boulder City Town Company to Nicholas Connelly Intst No. 19, Share No. 3
Share No. 4 not recorded; (block 9, lot 12 without a house is already listed to Goss, Pell & Lowe)

Interest No. 20

11 Aug 1859, Wm Cheatly [Cheatley] lots drawn; block 95, lot 8 with house to Leonidas Mitchel, Sylvester Hill (block 95 lot 8 not listed in the September list)

block	lot	block	lot	block	lot	block	lot
96	2	117	10	42	1	60	7
117	1	100	8	41	12	114	8
156	11	123	6	13	3	92	4
48	12	150	2	171	8	6	6
173	3	[95]	[8]				

20 Sept 1859, Boulder City Town Company to Boulder City Association Interest No. 20, Share No. 1

Shares 2-4 not recorded; (block 60, lot 7 already listed to Charles B Akins)

Interest No. 21

11 Aug 1859, M D Cowsert lots drawn

block	lot	block	lot	block	lot	block	lot
70	7	117	9	41	4	59	11
118	6	100	9	116	6	117	2
154	8	146	7	13	4	92	3
48	6	149	5	172	8	6	7
173	4		(only 17 lots recorded)				

3 April 1861, Boulder City Town Company to M D Cowsert Interest No. 21, Share No. 1

Interest No. 22

11 Aug 1859, John Cassity [Cassidy] lots drawn, transferred to M D Cowsert, then transferred to Goss, Pell & Lowe; block 99, lot 10 to E C Thompson; block 70, lot 3, George Hoole (no lots listed on 20 Sept, all lots listed 11 August)

block	lot	block	lot	block	lot	block	lot
66	12	99	10	70	3	62	2
163	7	58	3	102	1	104	2

block	lot	block	lot	block	lot	block	lot
107	2	38	12	15	9	17	3
175	12	50	8	167	9	169	1
168	4	(only 17 lots listed)					

no date, Boulder City Town Company to Goss, Pell & Lowe Interest No. 22, Share No. 1
Shares 2-4 not recorded

Interest No. 23

11 Aug 1859, C M Clouser lots drawn; block 95, lot 10 with house transferred to D Parlin, then transferred to D Pound; block 54, lot 12 (not listed below) to E Donnelly

block	lot	block	lot	block	lot	block	lot
95	10	65	12	99	5	70	11
61	10	151	7	114	9	101	6
111	8	158	2	39	12	15	4
17	9	4	6	51	2	168	9
167	1	169	4	[54]	[12]		

16 March 1863, Boulder City Town Company to C M Clouser Interest No. 23, Share No. 1
Shares 2-4 not recorded; (block 114, lot 9 already listed to Buell & Donnelly)

Interest No. 24

11 Aug 1859, Louis G Davenport lots drawn, 1/2 transferred to A Barker by D M ___oly, Agent; 1/2 to Wm Vandiver; block 95, lot 4 with house to A Barker; block 92, lot 8 from A Barker to S Whitney; **20 Sept 1859**, William Vandiver to A Barker, 1/2 Interest No. 24

block	lot	block	lot	block	lot	block	lot
96	8	63	3	41	1	61	3
122	1	102	11	42	7	113	10
95	4	157	10	124	12	13	11
92	8	49	7	151	3	170	9
167	7	172	2				

6 Oct 1860, Boulder City Town Company to A Barker Interest No. 24, Share No. 1
Share 2 not recorded

6 Oct 1860, Boulder City Town Company to A Barker Interest No. 24, Share No. 3
Share 4 not recorded; (block 157, lot 10 already listed to M W Towner)

20 Sept 1859, William Vandiver to A Barker, 1/2 Interest No. 24[, including the following lots:]

block	lot	block	lot	block	lot	block	lot
96	8	63	3	61	3	122	1
42	7	113	10	95	4	157	10
151	3	170	9				

20 Sept 1859, A Barker to William Vandiver, Interest No. 24, share No. 4 and 1/2 share No. 2, including the following lots:

block	lot	block	lot	block	lot	block	lot
96	8	102	11	124	12	49	7
172	2	41	1	13	11	167	7

Interest No. 25

11 Aug 1859, George Dixon lots drawn, transferred to Charles N Easner, transferred from Easner to Albert Corbin; 1/4 interest transferred by Dixon to Sears, Whitely, Chapman, Baugh & Hamilton on **21 July 1859**; block 69, lot 5 to L L Locklin (crossed out for Horace Annis) (no lots listed on 20 Sept, all listed on 11 Aug)

block	lot	block	lot	block	lot	block	lot
69	5	118	10	64	9	44	4
59	6	120	4	43	10	114	7
113	2	112	5	111	1	46	5
47	4	151	1	145	5	173	10
11	12	176	3				

No date, Boulder City Town Company to George Dixon Interest No. 25, Share No. 1
Shares 2-4 not recorded
(the block and lot numbers transferred to Sears, Whitely, Chapman, Baugh & Hamilton not
     recorded)
(block 43, lot 10 already listed to W G Pell; block 111, lot 1 already listed to Goss, Pell &
     Lowe; block 118, lot 10 already listed to David Stone & Co)

Interest No. 26

11 Aug 1859, D [Denison] J Ely lots drawn, transferred to Franklin Winslow 12 Apr 1859

block	lot	block	lot	block	lot	block	lot
96	5	65	3	41	6	59	8
118	4	101	9	40	12	114	11
156	8	124	1	13	9	92	10
49	12	150	5	171	11	168	7
172	4			(Only 17 lots recorded)			

18 April 1859 [probably 1860], Boulder City Town Company to Franklin Winslow Interest No. 26, Share No. 1

Shares 2-4 not recorded

Interest No. 27

11 Aug 1859, O [Oliver] P Goodwin lots drawn, block 122, lot 11 (not listed on 20 Sept list); block 68, lot 1 (not listed in the 11 Aug list)

block	lot	block	lot	block	lot	block	lot
116	7	45	3	61	6	119	3
100	4	111	6	115	3	152	9
17	12	46	8	124	11	147	6
147	3	178	8	9	1	145	10
68	1	[122]	[11]				

3 April 1861, Boulder City Town Company to O P Goodwin Interest No. 27, Share No. 1
Shares 2-4 not recorded

Interest No. 28

11 Aug 1859, S D Hotchkiss interest transferred to M D Cowsart [Cowsert], then transferred to Goss, Pell & Lowe on 30 July 1859, lots drawn; block 118, lot 7 to Geo Hoole (no lots listed on 20 Sept)

block	lot	block	lot	block	lot	block	lot
95	1	118	7	43	2	43	4
120	1	59	3	41	10	115	1

block	lot	block	lot	block	lot	block	lot
12	3	111	2	46	6	13	5
58	11	153	6	178	10	174	11
146	11	178	2				

no date, Boulder City Town Company to Goss, Pell & Lowe Interest No. 28, Share No. 1
Shares 2-4 not recorded
(block 95, lot 1 previously listed to M D Cowsert with a house)

Interest No. 29

11 Aug 1859, David Horsefall [Horsfal] lots drawn, transferred to Wm Sargent; D Horsefall [Horsfal] transferred block 67, lot 12 to Alvah Fay (not listed below, has a house)

block	lot	block	lot	block	lot	block	lot
65	6	150	7	158	4	4	12
170	2	99	3	104	11	71	7
50	3	70	9	101	12	14	8
168	11	60	8	111	10	71	8
166	1	[67]	[12]				

no date, Boulder City Town Company to David Horsefall [Horsfal] Interest No. 29, Share No. 1
Shares 2-4 not recorded
(block 65, lot 6 already listed with a building to Wm M Barney; block 99, lot 3 already listed to P G Cooper)

Interest No. 30

11 Aug 1859, A [Addison] W Harris lots drawn, transferred to George W Horton; block 52, lot 3 (not listed below) transferred from A W Harris to J L Scherrer & Co

block	lot	block	lot	block	lot	block	lot
66	7	99	9	70	4	62	3
152	12	58	4	102	7	104	3
157	3	39	6	15	8	17	2
178	7	50	9	167	10	169	6

| 168 | 5 | 119 | 12 | [52] | [3] |

block 119, lot 12 had a **house**
20 Sept 1859, Boulder City Town Company to A W Harris Interest No. 30, Share No. 1
Shares 2-4 not recorded; (block 66, lot 7 already listed to B A Sinn)

Interest No. 31

11 Aug 1859, George Hackelman interest transferred to M W Towner **2 May 1859**, lots drawn; 1/4 transferred to Theodore Squires; 1/4 transferred to T R Hamilton; block 121, lot 9, block 96, lot 9, block 157, lot 9, block 151, lot 4 to Thomas & Williams

block	lot	block	lot	block	lot	block	lot
96	9	63	4	40	6	61	4
147	12	102	10	43	12	113	9
157	9	124	7	14	5	71	2
50	1	151	4	40	11	166	12
171	5	121	9				

20 Sept 1859, Boulder City Town Company to M W Towner Interest No. 31, Share No. 1
Shares 2-4 not recorded; (1/4 interest to Theodore Squires no block and lot numbers listed; 1/4 interest to T R Hamilton blockand lot numbers not listed)

Interest No. 32

11 Aug 1859, John R Hall lots drawn, select blocks assigned to A M Hunt and Jas Boutwell

block	lot	block	lot	block	lot	block	lot
69	9	103	8	103	1	15	6
48	5	176	6				

Blocks Assigned to A M Hunt

65	10	63	7	122	5	156	6
132	5	38	9	16	2	170	7
165	4	51	10				

Block Assigned to Jas Boutwell

98	5

No date, Boulder City Town Company to Jno R Hall Interest No. 32, Share No. 1
Shares 2-4 not recorded

Interest No. 33

11 Aug 1859, T [Thaddeus] R Hamilton lots drawn, transferred to W S Edson, W B Edson, & O Rogers; block 69, lot 6 transferred to M W Towner (no lots listed on 20 Sept, all listed on 11 Aug)

block	lot	block	lot	block	lot	block	lot
69	6	67	8	99	12	93	8
62	4	153	12	150	8	154	12
103	4	156	4	38	7	15	11
39	9	176	12	49	10	167	9
170	1	168	2				

10 Aug 1860, T R Hamilton to W S Edson, W B Edson, O Rogers Intst No. 33, Share No. 1
10 Aug 1860, T R Hamilton to W S Edson, W B Edson, O Rogers Intst No. 33, Share No. 2
10 Aug 1860, T R Hamilton to W S Edson, W B Edson, O Rogers Intst No. 33, Share No. 3
10 Aug 1860, T R Hamilton to W S Edson, W B Edson, O Rogers Intst No. 33, Share No. 4
(block 167, lot 9 already listed to Goss, Pell & Lowe)

Interest No. 34

11 Aug 1859, Wm K Hughey lots drawn; declared void by the Board of Directors **2 July 1860**

block	lot	block	lot	block	lot	block	lot
68	8	98	11	93	12	62	10
58	12	149	11	156	7	102	3
154	3	16	6	38	5	17	4
173	7	49	3	166	8	173	6
166	4		(only 17 lots recorded)				

No date, Boulder City Town Company to Wm K Hughey Interest No. 34, Share No. 1
No date, Boulder City Town Company to Wm K Hughey Interest No. 34, Share No. 2
20 Sept 1859, Boulder City Town Company to William K Hughey, Intst No. 34, share No. 2
20 Sept 1859, Boulder City Town Company to William K Hughey, Intst No. 34, share No. 3
20 Sept 1859, Boulder City Town Company to William K Hughey, Intst No. 34, share No. 4
2 May 1860, Wm K Hughey transferred to James H Russell Interest No. 34, Share No. 1
11 July 1860, J [James] H Russell transferred to Henry A Newman Interest No. 34, Share No. 1, witnesses J H Decker, H C Norton

Interest No. 35

11 Aug 1859, W [William] W Jones lots drawn (no lots listed on 20 Sept, all listed 11 Aug)

block	lot	block	lot	block	lot	block	lot
96	4	117	12	41	3	59	9
122	1	40	7	114	10	156	9
123	12	13	8	92	11	49	1
150	4	171	10	5	12	172	5
101	10		(only 17 lots recorded)				

No date, Boulder City Town Company to W W Jones Interest No. 35, Share No. 1
Shares 2-4 not recorded; (block 122, lot 1 already listed to A Barker)

Interest No. 36

11 Aug 1859, Thomas Lorton (crossed out), A F Kennedy lots drawn (no lots listed on 20 Sept, all listed 11 Aug)

block	lot	block	lot	block	lot	block	lot
19	8	64	6	44	2	59	7
121	2	115	8	113	7	114	4
151	10	12	1	46	3	47	2
150	1	146	3	173	8	11	6
176	5		(only 17 lots recorded)				

no date, Boulder City Town Company to George W Thorp Interest No. 36, Share No. 1
Share no 2 not recorded
28 Dec 1859, G W Thorp transferred to Chas Eyser Interest No. 36, Share No. 3
13 Dec 1859, G W Thorp transferred to Frederick Bohnens Interest No. 36, Share No. 4

Interest No. 37

11 Aug 1859, Thomas Lorton transferred to A A Brookfield, then 1/2 interest to George Dixon 30 April 1859 then lots drawn; G [George] Dixon transferred 1/4 interest to Baugh, Hamilton & Co; block 69, lot 12 transferred from AAB [Alfred A Brookfield] to LL Locklin to Lois [Louis] J Walling

Lots transferred from L L Locklin to A A Brookfield

block	lot	block	lot	block	lot	block	lot
69	4	65	8	63	8	103	12
98	2	152	2	98	1	39	4
48	2	6	3*				

Lots transferred from A A Brookfield to L L Locklin

block	lot	block	lot	block	lot	block	lot
69	12	103	11	122	12	158	6
16	5	168	12	166	5	178	1
6	3*						

17 Mar 1860, Boulder City Town Company to George Dixon Interest No. 37, Share No. 1
17 Mar 1860, Boulder City Town Company to George Dixon Interest No. 37, Share No. 2
Shares 3-4 not recorded; (block 103, lot 11 already listed to T J Jones and Redener; block 122, lot 12 with a house already listed to Bicknel, Cook, Hotchkiss & Buckwalter)

*1/2

Interest No. 38

11 Aug 1859, John McKay lots drawn, transferred to I [Isaac] S Bull [Buell]; then from Isaac S Bull [Buell] to John L Buell; and from Jno L Buell to Davidson Breath & Co (no lots listed on 20 Sept, all listed on 11 Aug)

block	lot	block	lot	block	lot	block	lot
120	9	94	1	117	7	45	5
57	2	119	5	100	2	112	6
153	11	17	6	45	10	134	9
146	6	145	5	176	10	8	6
173	4	116	5				

No date, Boulder City Town Company to Davidson & Breath Interest No. 38, Share No. 1 (Golden City)
Shares 2-4 not recorded; (block 120, lot 9 with house already listed to John L Buell, block 173, lot 4 already listed to M D Cowsert, block 145, lot 5 already listed to Albert Corbin)

Interest No. 39

11 Aug 1859, Alfred Miller lots drawn, transferred to Cook, Bicknel & Buckwalter; block 122, lot 12 with house (not listed below); block 68, lot 12 transferred from Buckwalter to D Parlin; block 101, lot 3 transferred from Buckwalter to D Parlin

block	lot	block	lot	block	lot	block	lot
68	12	66	8	93	2	62	8
104	7	148	10	157	6	101	3
153	5	14	1	38	11	16	9
171	7	48	10	165	8	175	6
51	8	[122]	[12]				

No date, Boulder City Town Company to W S Buckwalter No. 39, Share No. 1
Shares 2-4 not recorded; (block 153, lot 5 already listed to Alfred A Brookfield)

Interest No. 40

11 Aug 1859, W [William] B Moore lots drawn, transferred to Robert Mc-Farland

block	lot	block	lot	block	lot	block	lot
65	5	149	12	158	5	51	6
170	3	99	6	103	8	71	1
51	11	70	8	100	7	14	9
169	11	60	9	111	11	71	9
166	6	(only 17 lots recorded)					

20 Sept 1859, Boulder City Town Company to Robert McFarland Intst No. 40, Share No. 1
Shares 2-4 not recorded; (block 65, lot 5 already listed to T J Jones & Redener; block 103, lot 8 already listed to John R Hall)

Interest No. 41

11 Aug 1859, J P McChesney lots drawn, transferred to Theodore Squires

block	lot	block	lot	block	lot	block	lot
168	3	67	7	99	11	70	2
62	1	150	9	58	2	102	6

block	lot	block	lot	block	lot	block	lot
103	5	156	5	38	1	15	10
39	8	175	7	49	11	167	10
170	6	(only 17 lots recorded)					

10 Feb 1863, Boulder City Town Company to Theodore Squires Interest No. 41, Share No. 1 Shares 2-4 not recorded; (block 167, lot 10 already listed to George W Horton)

Interest No. 42

11 Aug 1859, Dennis McMannis [McManus] lots drawn, transferred to George W Nichols, 5 Sept [1859]

block	lot	block	lot	block	lot	block	lot
94	2	64	2	45	1	60	12
118	2	42	11	112	1	116	4
153	10	17	1	45	9	124	8
146	1	148	4	176	9	7	1
175	5	94	5				

No date, Boulder City Town Company to George W Nichols Interest No. 42, Share No. 1 Shares 2-4 not recorded

Interest No. 43

11 Aug 1859, Jno [John] Moran transferred to David S Corbin 24 April 1859 then lots drawn; block 116, lot 11 transferred from Wm Parks then to Wm Mills; block 119, lot 6 transferred to D P [probably Daniel Pound]; block 114, lot 6 to Wm Parks (no lots listed on 20 Sept, all on 11 Aug)

block	lot	block	lot	block	lot	block	lot
95	2	93	7	116	11	42	5
60	4	119	6	100	11	114	6
117	4	154	10	145	7	44	9
124	5	47	12	149	3	175	9
6	12	174	5				

No date, Boulder City Town Company to David S Corbin Interest No. 43, Share No. 1 Shares 2-4 not recorded

Interest No. 44

11 Aug 1859, A B Parrington [Perrington] lots drawn, transferred block 121, lot 12 with a house to Franklin Mayse [Mays]; interest 44 sold for taxes 10 Sept 1859, redeemed 14 Sept 1859

block	lot	block	lot	block	lot	block	lot
121	12	69	10	98	12	103	9
63	10	103	6	122	4	158	1
98	4	152	4	158	7	38	8
16	3	169	12	48	4	165	3
176	1	6	5				

No date, Boulder City Town Company to A B Perrington Interest No. 44, Share No. 1 Shares 2-4 not recorded; (block 103, lot 9 already listed to P G Cooper)

Interest No. 45

11 Aug 1859, John Rotherick [Rothrock] lots drawn; block 69, lot 1 transferred to Anthony Arnett; block 93, lot 11 transferred to S Whitney (no lots listed on 20 Sept, all listed on 11 Aug)

block	lot	block	lot	block	lot	block	lot
69	1	68	7	98	10	93	11
62	11	58	7	149	10	156	12
102	4	154	4	16	2	147	11
39	3	173	12	49	4	166	9
172	1	167	2				

No date, Boulder City Town Company to John Rotheric [Rothrock] Intst No. 45, Share No. 1 Shares 2-4 not recorded; (block 16, lot 2 already listed to A M Hunt)

Interest No. 46

11 Aug 1859, R L Simpson lots drawn

block	lot	block	lot	block	lot	block	lot
119	9	64	5	43	6	60	1
121	3	115	9	112	7	114	3
151	9	13	12	46	2	123	2

block	lot	block	lot	block	lot	block	lot
149	6	146	4	172	11	10	1
175	2		(only 17 lots recorded)				

No date, Boulder City Town Company to R L Simpson Interest No. 46, Share No. 1
Shares 2-4 not recorded

Interest No. 47

11 Aug 1859, B A Sinn lots drawn; block 96, lot 10 to Jno [John] L Buell; block 63, lot 6 to Jn W Warren; block 61, lot 5 (not listed on 20 Sept, is listed on 11 Aug); block 115, lot 5 and block 122, lot 7 (listed on 20 Sept, not listed on 11 Aug)

block	lot	block	lot	block	lot	block	lot
96	10	63	6	40	5	115	5
147	7	102	9	43	7	113	8
157	8	92	1	14	4	71	3
50	12	151	5	170	10	166	7
171	4	122	7				

No date, Boulder City Town Company to B A Sinn, Interest No. 47, Share No. 1
Shares 2-4 not recorded; (block 115, lot 5 already listed to Edward Donnelly)

Interest No. 48

11 Aug 1859, Wm Scourfield lots drawn; block 95, lot 12 transferred to M D Cowsart, then to D Pound; block 68, lot 1 (listed on 20 Sept, not listed on 11 Aug)

block	lot	block	lot	block	lot	block	lot
65	3	99	2	40	2	61	12
149	7	103	10	100	9	112	9
158	9	92	6	14	11	71	11
51	1	50	4	169	9	165	6
170	5	68	1	95	12		

3 Apr 1861, Boulder City Town Company to Wm Scourfield Interest No. 48, Share No. 1
Shares 2-4 not recorded; (block 68, lot 1 already listed to O P Goodwin; block 65, lot 3 already listed to Franklin Winslow; block 100, lot 9 already listed to M D Cowsert); 19 lots recorded

Interest No. 49

11 Aug 1859, Theodore Squires lots drawn, transferred to Wm Mills **12 Sept 1859**; block 68, lot 6 to M W Towner (no lots listed 20 Sept, all listed on 11 Aug)

block	lot	block	lot	block	lot	block	lot
68	6	65	1	63	5	40	4
60	11	148	7	102	8	44	12
112	11	158	11	92	12	14	3
71	4	50	6	51	5	170	11
165	12	171	3				

No date, Boulder City Town Company to Theodore Squires Interest No. 49, Share No. 1
Shares 2-4 not recorded

Interest No. 50

11 Aug 1859, J P [Patrick J] Fray lots drawn, transferred to C M Clouser; 1/2 from C M Clouser to G W Thorp & Franklin Winslow

block	lot	block	lot	block	lot	block	lot
70	6	117	8	41	5	60	5
118	1	100	10	116	1	117	3
154	9	146	12	44	8	92	2
48	6	149	5	175	8	6	1
173	5		(only 17 lots recorded)				

26 Apr 1859 [probably 1860], Patric[k] J Fray to C M Clouser Interest No. 50, Share No. 1
Shares 2-4 not recorded; (1/2 transferred to Thorp & Winslow no block and lot numbers recorded, all lots listed as C M Clouser); (block 48, lot 6 already listed to M D Cowsert; block 110, lot 10 already listed to T J Jones and Redener; block 149, lot 5 already listed to M D Cowsert)

Interest No. 51

11 Aug 1859, M [Marquis] W Towner lots drawn; block 68, lot 5 Towner to Jameson [Jamison] & Jameson [Jamison], then to J Maxwell

block	lot	block	lot	block	lot	block	lot
93	6	42	8	44	10	7	6

block	lot	block	lot	block	lot	block	lot
116	10	114	1	124	4	174	4
42	4	117	5	47	7	68	5
60	3	154	11	149	2	119	1
145	12	175	10				

20 Sept 1859, Boulder City Town Company to M W Towner Interest No. 51, Share No. 1
Shares 2-4 not recorded

Interest No. 52

11 Aug 1859, J E Williams lots drawn, transferred to Daniel Blocher; block 121, lot 8 with house from D Blocher to W Mills (no lots listed on 20 Sept, all listed on 11 Aug)

block	lot	block	lot	block	lot	block	lot
121	8	118	9	64	11	43	1
121	1	59	5	41	8	115	7
113	5	111	4	46	12	12	3
58	9	152	6	145	2	174	9
146	9	178	4				

No date, Boulder City Town Company to Daniel Blocher Interest No. 52, Share No. 1
Shares 2-4 not recorded; (block 12, lot 3 already listed to Goss, Pell & Lowe)

Interest No. 53

11 Aug 1859, James Wagstaff lots drawn (no lots lsited on 20 Sept, all listed on 11 Aug)

block	lot	block	lot	block	lot	block	lot
68	9	66	11	93	5	62	9
100	12	46	1	157	12	102	2
154	2	14	7	38	4	17	5
172	12	49	2	165	11	173	1
166	3	(only 17 lots recorded)					

No date, Boulder City Town Company to James Wagstaff Interest No. 53, Share No. 1
Shares 2-4 not recorded

Interest No. 54

11 Aug 1859, Daniel Wagstaff lots drawn; block 122, lot 9 (listed on 20 Sept, not listed on 11 Aug)

block	lot	block	lot	block	lot	block	lot
66	5	99	8	70	12	61	8
152	7	58	5	102	12	104	4
157	4	39	7	15	2	17	11
178	12	50	10	167	11	168	1
169	2	122	9				

No date, Boulder City Town Company to G W Nichols Interest No. 54, Share No. 1
Shares 2-4 not recorded

Interest No. 55

11 Aug 1859, E S Warren lots drawn, transferred to J R Parker, then to J & C H Enos, then to Daniel Pound (no lots listed on 20 Sept, all listed on 11 Aug); all listed to D P [Daniel Pound]

block	lot	block	lot	block	lot	block	lot
67	3	69	7	65	9	103	10
63	9	103	7	122	3	158	12
98	3	152	3	98	6	39	5
16	4	169	7	48	3	165	2
178	6	6	4				

No date, Boulder City Town Company to S E [E S] Warren Interest No. 55, Share No. 1
Shares 2-4 not recorded; (block 103, lot 10 already listed to William Scourfield, block 165, lot 2 already listed to E S Warren)

Interest No. 56

11 Aug 1859, G [George] R Williamson lots drawn (no lots listed on 20 Sept, all listed on 11 Aug)

block	lot	block	lot	block	lot	block	lot
94	7	116	8	45	6	50	2
118	3	42	10	113	6	116	3

block	lot	block	lot	block	lot	block	lot
153	9	145	6	45	8	124	2
47	1	148	3	176	8	7	12
174	2			(only 17 lots recorded)			

No date, Boulder City Town Company to G R Williamson Interest No. 56, Share No. 1
Shares 2-4 not recorded; (block 113, lot 6 already listed to Edward Donnelly)

Interest No. 57

11 Aug 1859, D [David] M Wooley lots drawn; 1/2 [interest] and 1/2 house and lot to Philo [Phil] Weston on **7 Sept 1859**; on **27 Sept 1859** transferred ½ interest, ½ house and block 120, lot 12 from Philo Weston to Mary Ann Weston; A A Brookfield transferred to Mary Ann Weston, 1/2 of house on block 120, lot 12 (no lots listed on 20 Sept, all listed on 11 Aug)

block	lot	block	lot	block	lot	block	lot
120	12	67	10	98	8	70	1
62	5	58	1	149	8	154	7
103	2	156	2	16	12	147	9
39	11	174	12	49	8	166	11
171	1	167	4				

No date, Boulder City Town Company to Mary Ann Weston Interest No. 57, Share No. 1
Shares 2-4 not recorded

Interest No. 58

11 Aug 1859, T J [J L] Younker lots drawn, sold for taxes to Jas B Ross on **10 Sept 1859**; transferred from Ross to Daniel Buell on **22 Sept 1860** (no lots listed on 20 Sept, all listed on 11 Aug)

block	lot	block	lot	block	lot	block	lot
120	11	64	1	45	2	60	1
119	2	100	5	111	7	115	4
152	10	13	1	46	9	123	5
148	1	147	4	178	9	10	?
145	9			(only 17 lots recorded)			

No share certificates recorded; (block 60, lot 1 already listed to R L Simpson)

Interest No. 59

11 Aug 1859, G W Thorp (no lots listed on 11 Aug or 20 Sept)

Interest No. 60

11 Aug 1859, J D Henderson (no lots listed on 11 Aug or 20 Sept)

Land Transfers

19 Aug 1859, M W Towner to T R Hamilton, 1/4 of Interest No. 31

19 Aug 1859, M W Towner to Boutwell & Holden, house on lot 6 block 68

19 Aug 1859, John R Hall to James Boutwell, lot 5 block 98

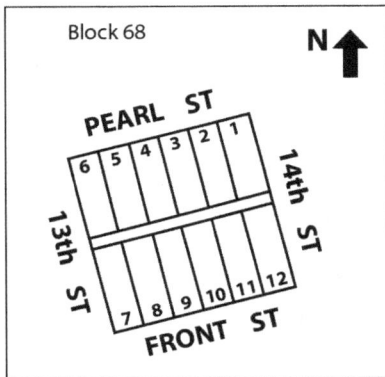

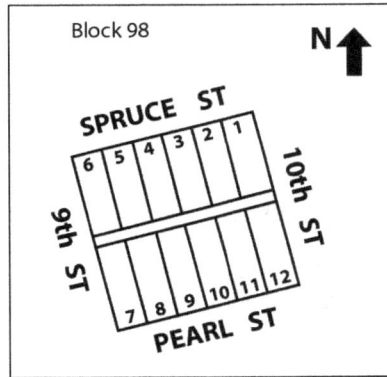

19 Aug 1859, T R Hamilton to M W Towner, house on lot 6 block 69

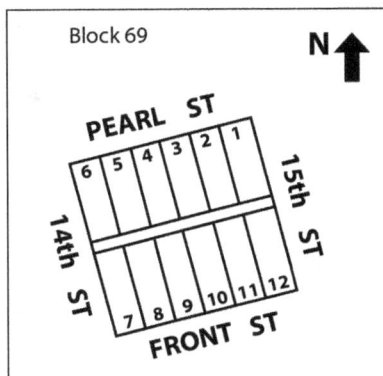

19 Aug 1859, John R Hall to A M Hunt, lot 10 block 65; lot 7 block 63; lot 5 block 122; lot 6 block 156; lot 5 block 152; lot 9 block 38; lot 2 block 16; lot 7 block 170; lot 4 block 165; lot 10 block 51

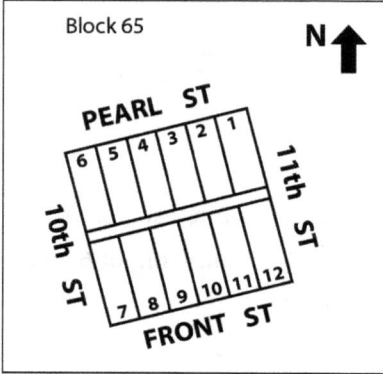

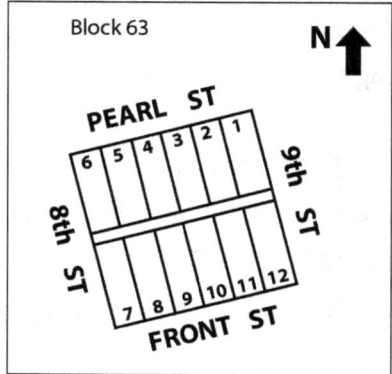

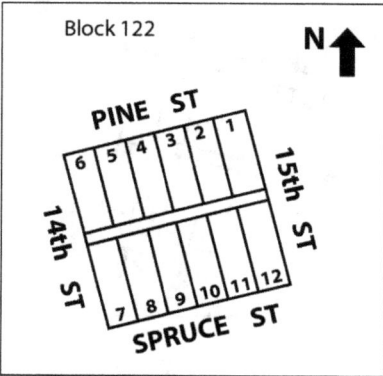

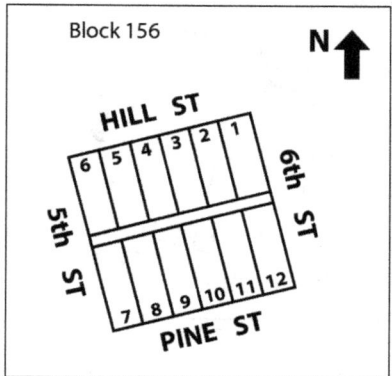

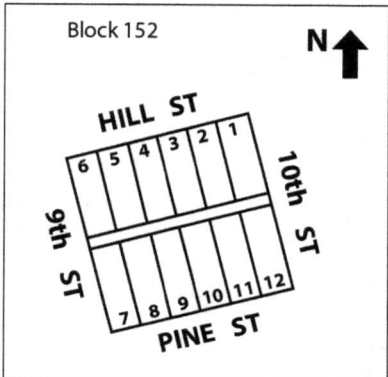

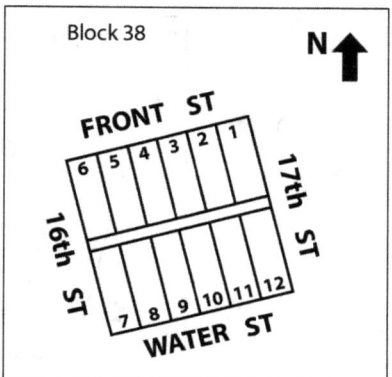

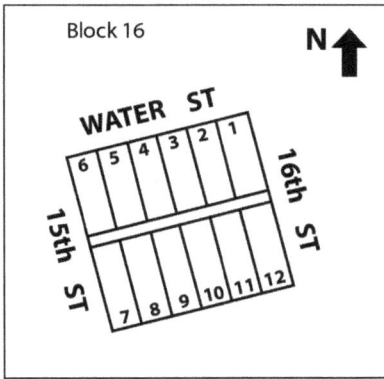

Block 16

WATER ST
6 5 4 3 2 1
15th ST
16th ST
7 8 9 10 11 12

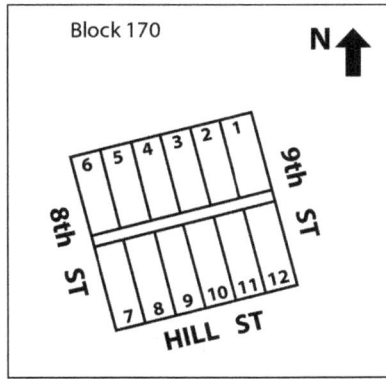

Block 170

4 3 2 1
6 5
8th ST
9th ST
7 8 9 10 11 12
HILL ST

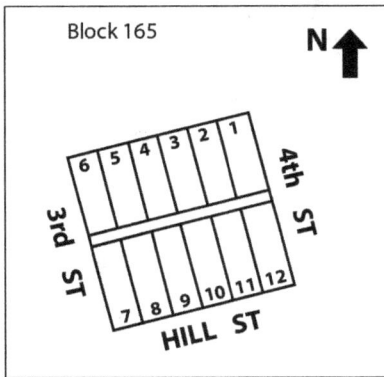

Block 165

6 5 4 3 2 1
3rd ST
4th ST
7 8 9 10 11 12
HILL ST

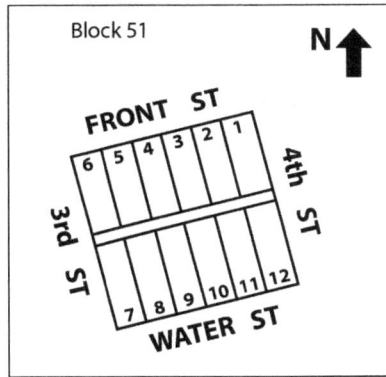

Block 51

FRONT ST
6 5 4 3 2 1
3rd ST
4th ST
7 8 9 10 11 12
WATER ST

1 Sept 1859, D and M Wooley (header, D M Wooley in the text), to Philo [Phil]Weston, 1/2 Interest No. 57 including 1/2 house on lot 12 block 120

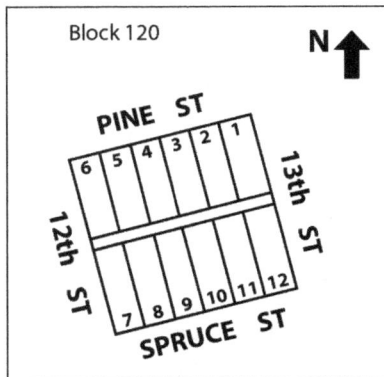

Block 120

PINE ST
6 5 4 3 2 1
12th ST
13th ST
7 8 9 10 11 12
SPRUCE ST

2 Sept 1859, Theodore Squires to William Mills, Interest No. 49, including house (no lot or block no)

3 Sept 1859, Dennis McMannus [McManus] to George W Nichols, Interest No. 42 including house (no lot or block no)

8 Sept 1859, B A Sinn to John L Buell, lot 7 block 99, lot 10 block 96

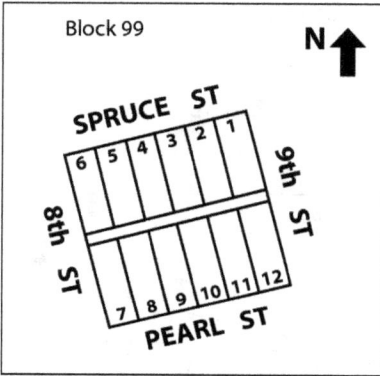

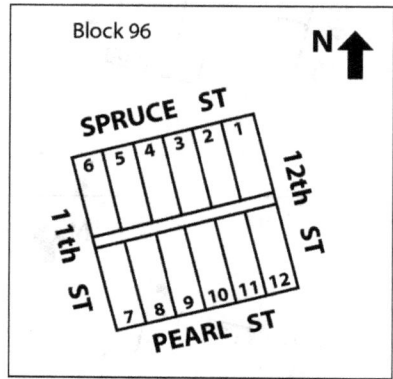

10 Sept 1859, E S Warren to J H Greenly, house on lot 4 block 67, lot 2 block 165

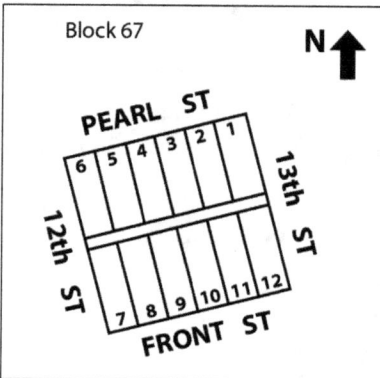

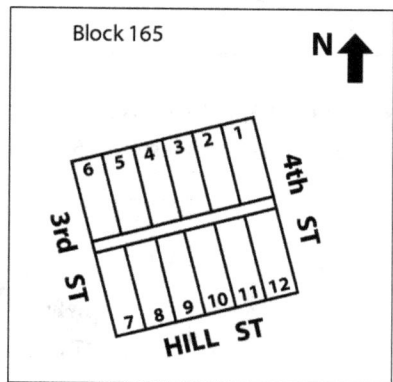

10 Sept 1859, David S Corbin failed to pay the taxes on Interest No. 14, sold to T J Jones.

10 Sept 1859, George Bicknel failed to pay taxes on Interest No. 15, sold to T J Jones

10 Sept 1859, George Bicknel failed to pay taxes on 1/4 of Interest No. 39, sold to T J Jones

10 Sept 1859, Charles E Cook failed to pay taxes on Interest No. 17, sold to T J Jones (John L Buell & E Donnelly in the header, T J Jones in the body)

10 Sept 1859, Albert Baber forfeited his interest, which was donated to J D Henderson

10 Sept 1859, W B Moore to Robert McFarland, all title and interest (Interest No. 40)

10 Sept 1859, J D Henderson for failure to pay taxes on Interest No. 11, sold to W G Pell

10 Sept 1859, Thomas Aikens [Akins] to Edward Donnelly, Interest No. 2

12 Sept 1859, M W Towner to J H Thomas & Isaac Williams, lot 9 block 96 (also listed to B A Sinn); lot 9 block 157; lot 4 block 151; house on lot 9 block 121

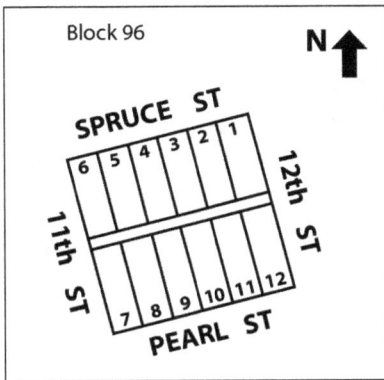

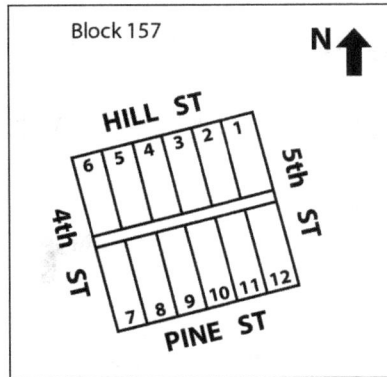

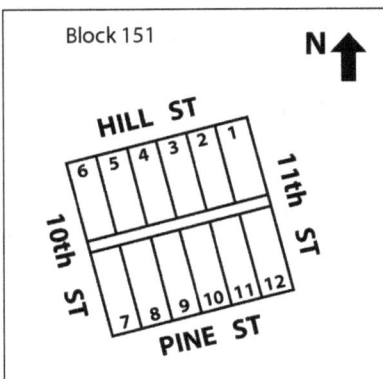

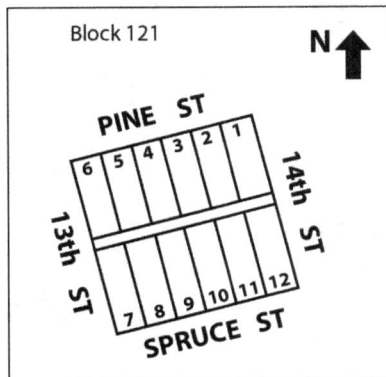

12 Sept 1859, John W Stokes has transferred interest No. 18 including the house on lot 6 block 95 to James Robinson and Huntwell S Tracy.

12 Sept 1859, John L Buell to Davidson, Breath & Co, Interest No. 38, including the house built upon lot no 9 in block 120

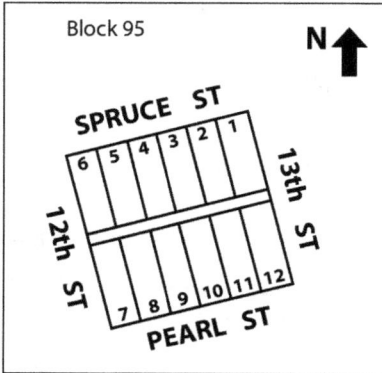

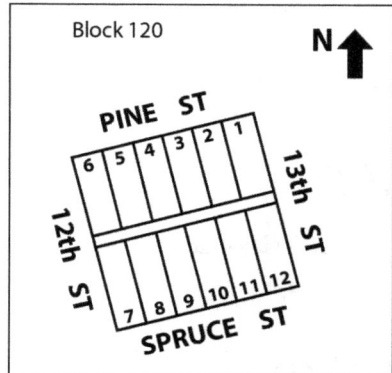

13 Sept 1859, William Cheatly by agent Daniel Bourlin to Leonidas Mitchel, block 95, lot 8, witness Jno L Buel [Buell]

14 Sept 1859, Daniel Blocker to William Mills, (house listed on this lot earlier) lot 8, block 121 belonging to Interest No. 52

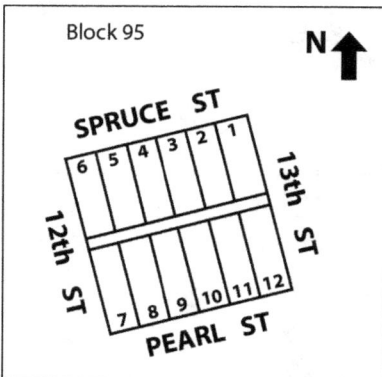

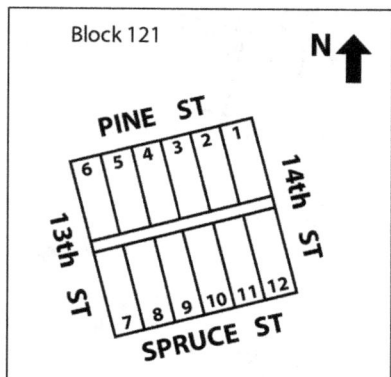

14 Sept 1859, Daniel Blocher to A C McBrian, lot 1 block 101, belonging to Interest No. 10, Share No. 1

14 Sept 1859, Nicholas Connelly to S W Tower, house on lot 12, block 94

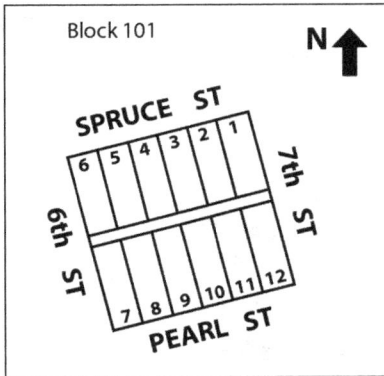

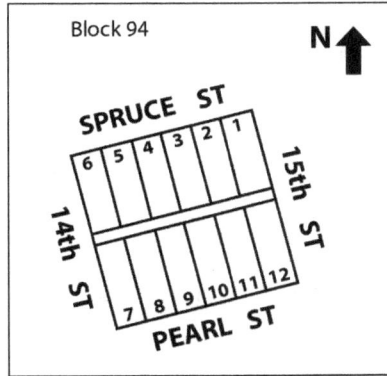

4 Sept 1859, William Cheatly, by his agent Daniel Blocher quit claims his interest in lot 8 block 95 to Leonidas Mitchell

14 Sept 1859, W B Moore to Robert McFarland, Interest No. 40 including House on Lot 10 Block 94

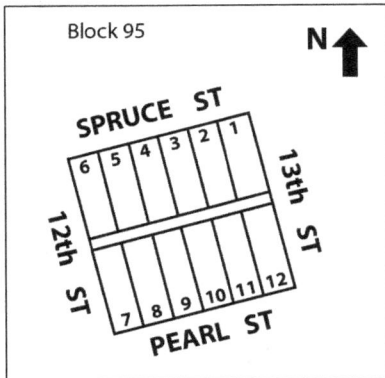

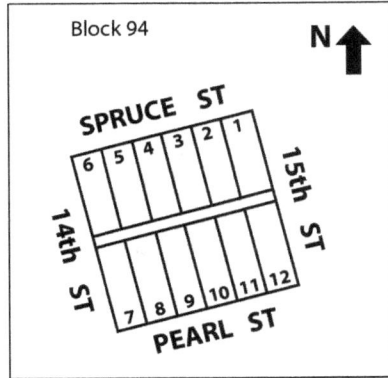

17 Sept 1859, James Abel to Daniel Williams, Interest No. 1 including house (no lot or block no)

19 Sept 1859, Edward Donnelly to Eli C Thompkins, house on lot 10 block 94 (listed earlier to W B Moore)

19 Sept 1859, David S Corbin to William Parks, lot 11 block 68; lot 9 block 66; lot 11 block 116; lot 6 block 114; lot 12 block 63; lot 4 block 101; house on lot 9 block 94

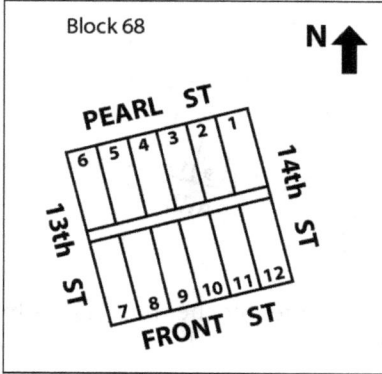

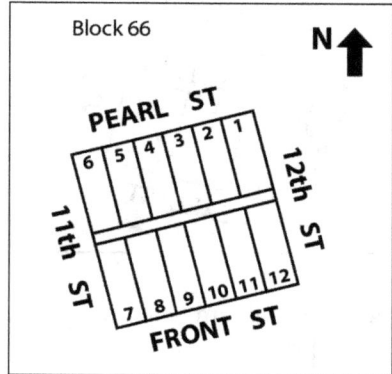

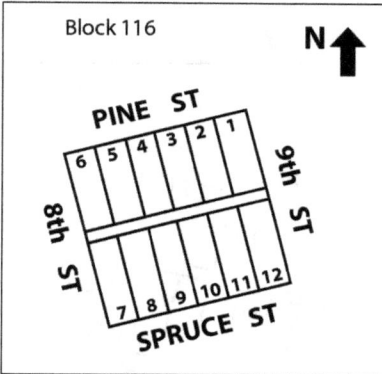

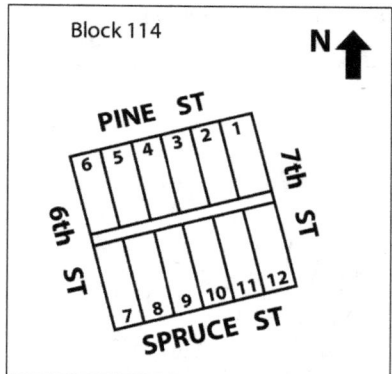

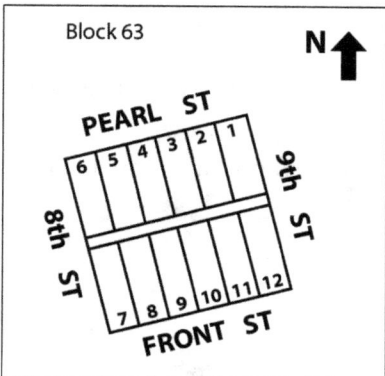

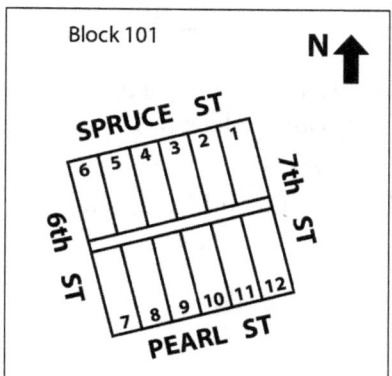

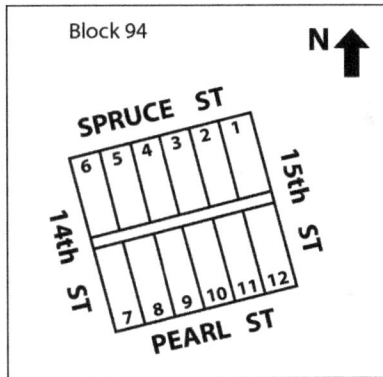

Block 94

20 Sept 1859, John L Buell to H F Crow & Henry Brindy, lot 10 block 96 (listed earlier to B A Sinn)

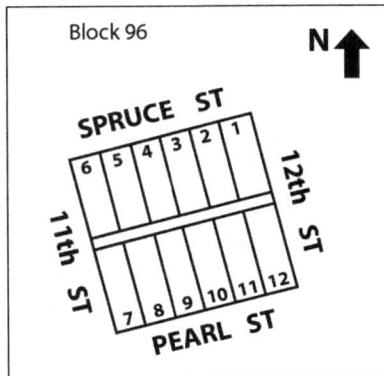

Block 96

20 Sept 1859, R L Simson [Simpson] to S W Tower, One Share of 18 lots (doesn't say what Interest No.), witness H C Norton, C J Goss, M D Cowsert

20 Sept 1859, Boulder City Town Company to Jas B Ross, Interest No. 58 for taxes, W B Edson, Recorder for J G Williams Jr, J C Goss, President, W S Buckwalter, Secy

20 Sept 1859, Goss, Pell & Lowe to George A Elle, lot 7 block 119; lot 12 block 12

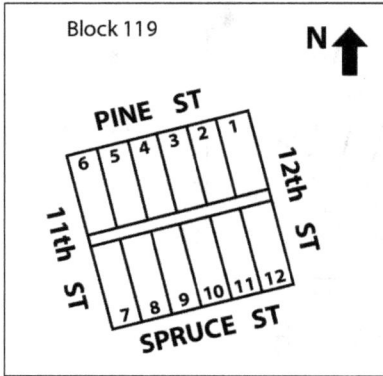

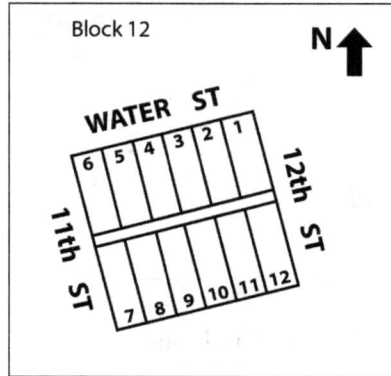

Block 119   N

PINE ST
6 5 4 3 2 1
11th ST   12th ST
7 8 9 10 11 12
SPRUCE ST

Block 12   N

WATER ST
6 5 4 3 2 1
11th ST   12th ST
7 8 9 10 11 12

20 Sept 1859, Goss, Pell & Lowe to George Hoole, lot 3 block 70; lot 7 block 118

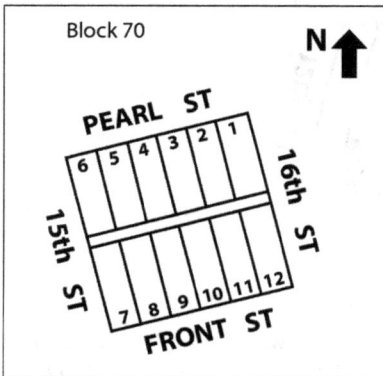

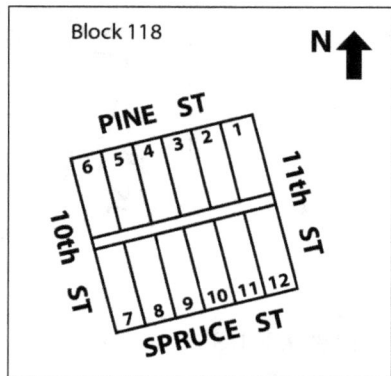

Block 70   N

PEARL ST
6 5 4 3 2 1
15th ST   16th ST
7 8 9 10 11 12
FRONT ST

Block 118   N

PINE ST
6 5 4 3 2 1
10th ST   11th ST
7 8 9 10 11 12
SPRUCE ST

26 Sept 1859, Rufus Trowbridge to H P Butler, house on lot 11 block 96, witness S E Stephenson

11 Oct 1859, George Dickson [Dixon] to L L Locklin, house on lot 4 block 66

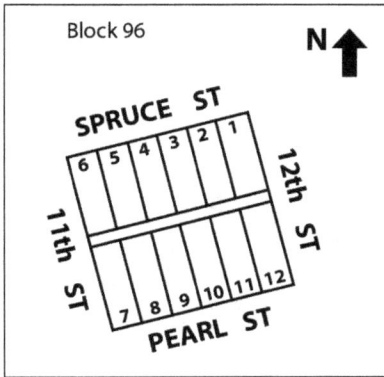

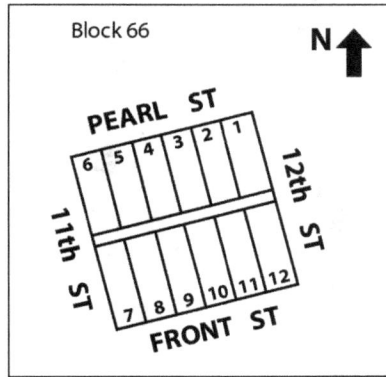

11 Oct 1859, J P B Irwin to Jas H Brown, Interest No. 20, share No. 4

18 Oct 1859, Jas H Brown to S R [P] Drew, Interest No. 20, share No. 4

18 Oct 1859, Franklin Winslow to S P Drew, Interest No. 26, share No. 4

18 Oct 1859, Thorp & Winslow to S P Drew, the following lots, Interest No. 7, shares No. 2 & 3:

block	lot	block	lot	block	lot	block	lot
122	12	68	2	99	4	70	10
150	12	104	10	111	9	15	5
51	3	169	5				

house on lot 12, block 122; **house** on lot 2, block 68

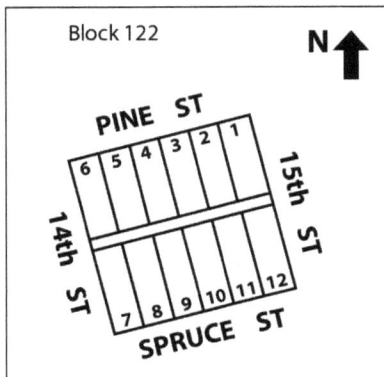

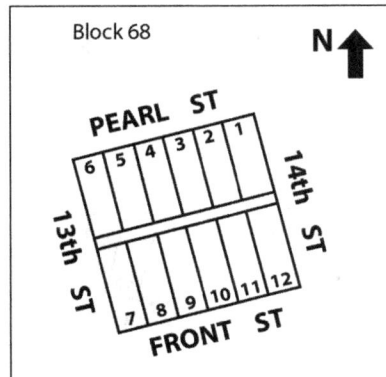

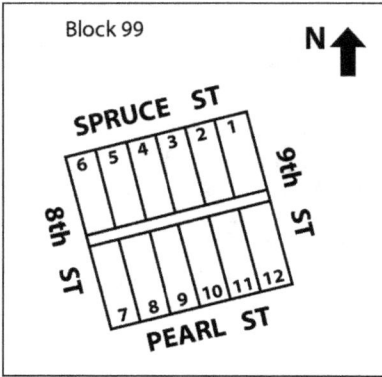

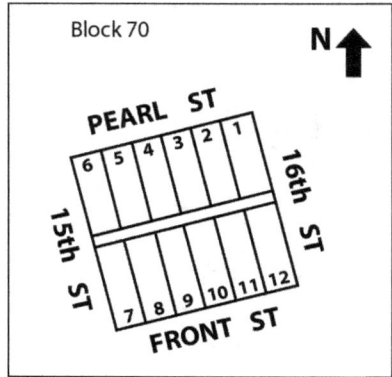

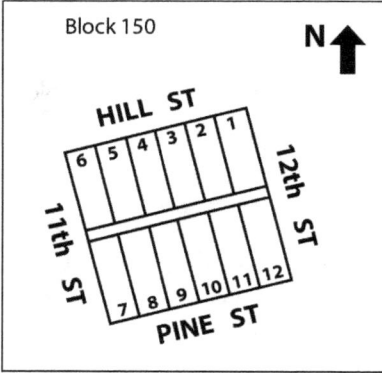

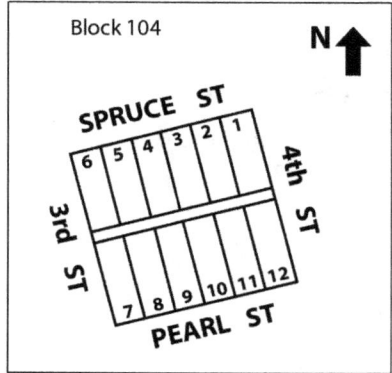

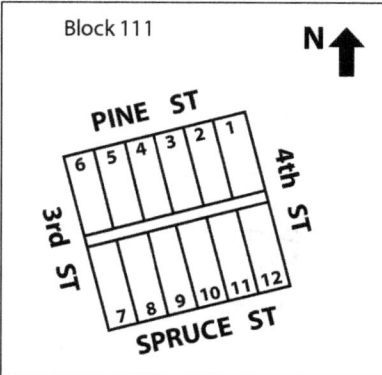

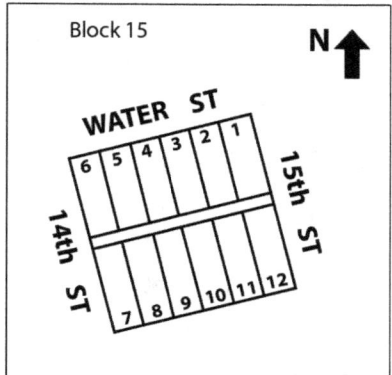

Block 99

SPRUCE ST
6 5 4 3 2 1
8th ST
9th ST
7 8 9 10 11 12
PEARL ST

Block 70

PEARL ST
6 5 4 3 2 1
15th ST
16th ST
7 8 9 10 11 12
FRONT ST

Block 150

HILL ST
6 5 4 3 2 1
11th ST
12th ST
7 8 9 10 11 12
PINE ST

Block 104

SPRUCE ST
6 5 4 3 2 1
3rd ST
4th ST
7 8 9 10 11 12
PEARL ST

Block 111

PINE ST
6 5 4 3 2 1
3rd ST
4th ST
7 8 9 10 11 12
SPRUCE ST

Block 15

WATER ST
6 5 4 3 2 1
14th ST
15th ST
7 8 9 10 11 12

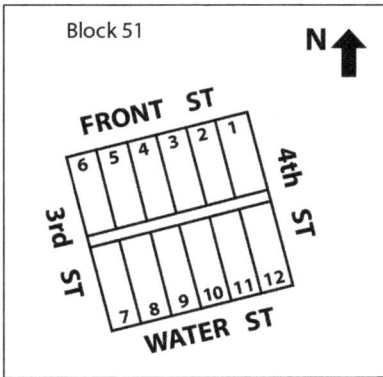

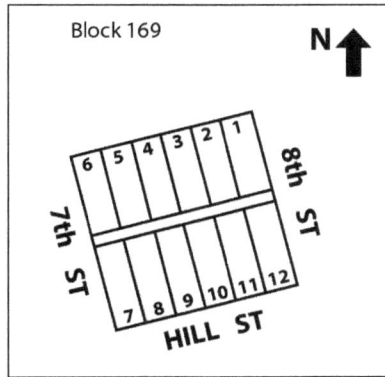

28 Oct 1859, Albert Corbin to M G Smith, lot 7, block 93; lot 2 block 95

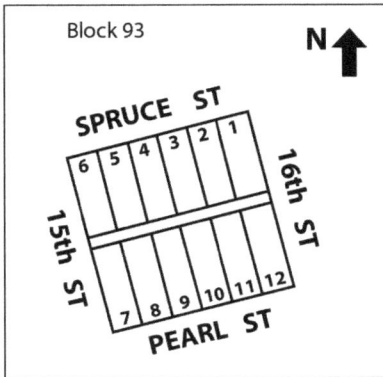

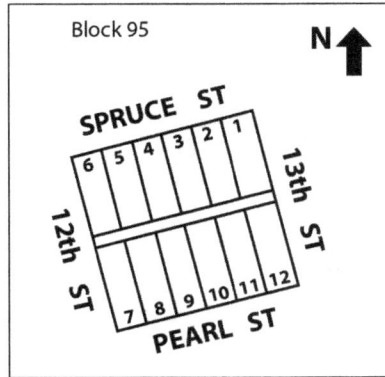

28 Oct 1859, Albert Corbin to Theodore Squires, Intst No. 43, share No. 4

4 Nov 1859, Charles B Aikins [Akins] assigned Interest No. 3 to H C Norton, and W V Boughton

7 Nov 1859, Edward Donnelly assigned Shares 1-4, Interest No. 2 to Thomas Aikins [Akins]

7 Nov 1859, Thomas Aikins [Akins] transferred to Edward Donnelly, block 64, lot 3, block 44, lot 6

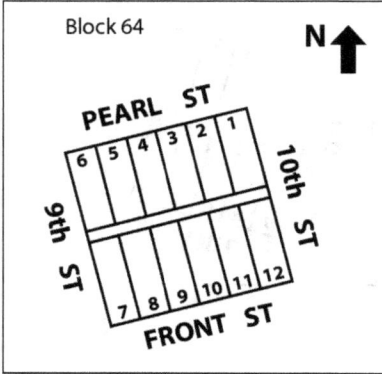

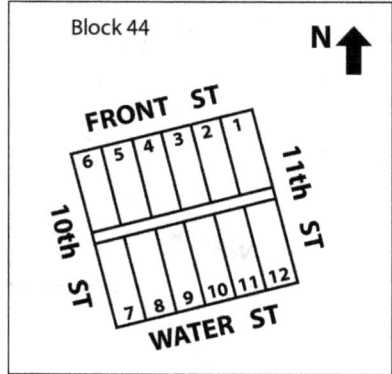

13 Nov 1859, M G Smith to Morse H Coffin, lot 7 block 93; lot 2 block 95

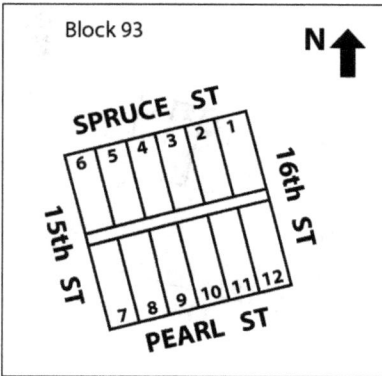

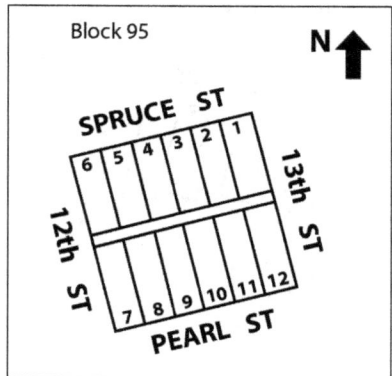

16 Nov 1859, William Parks to Phillip Quigler, lot 9 block 94

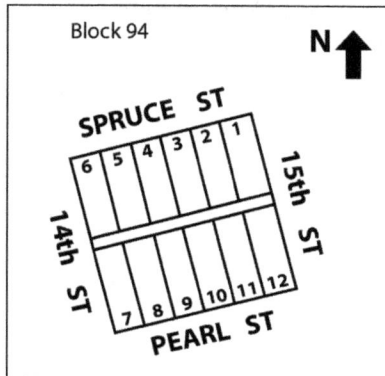

1860

18 Jan 1860, James B Ross of Moro, NM empowers Jno B P Irwin to lease, rent or sell 1/4 of his original Interest in the town of Golden City, one land claim adjoining Daniel McCleary's on Clear Creek, Arapahoe County. Also an original interest in Boulder City, Interest No. 58 being a tax title. Also three quartz claims on Gold Hill, Boulder Diggings, witnesses at Moro, NM, Gilbert Huntington, F A Roberts

23 Jan 1860, G W Thorp quitclaimed to T__d Brounculter (??), lot 7, block 96. Witnesses J Whitney, John Rothrock

10 Feb 1860, Boulder City Town company held its annual meeting at the W S Buckwalter House

17 Feb 1860, A Barker to J Whitney, lot 8 block 92, witness Robert Turner, R L Simpson

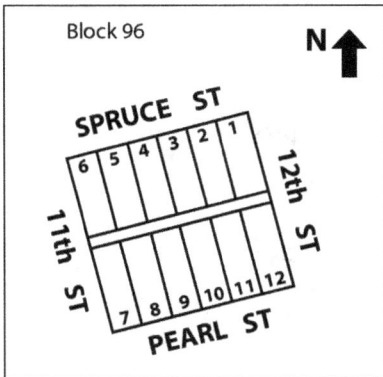

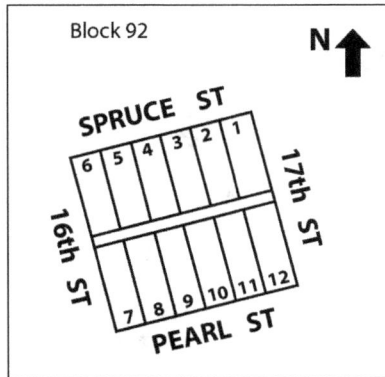

19 Mar 1860, L L Locklin to Lois [Louis] J Walling, lot 12 block 69, signed by L L Locklin and Mary Locklin, witness H C Norton

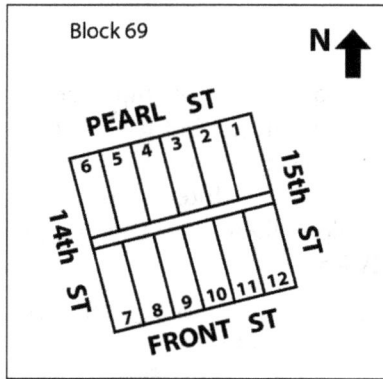

24 Mar 1860, Henry C Norton to James Roberson & Co (M H Coffin), lot 4 block 64; lot 10 block 115; lot 12 block 112; signed H C Norton and Harriett E Norton

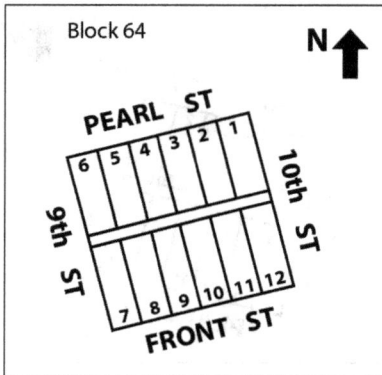

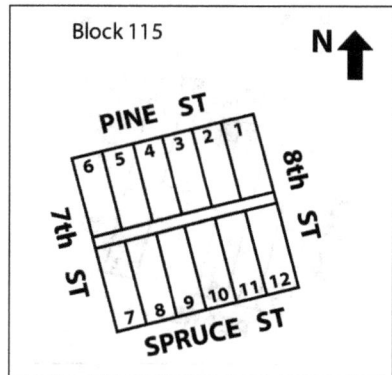

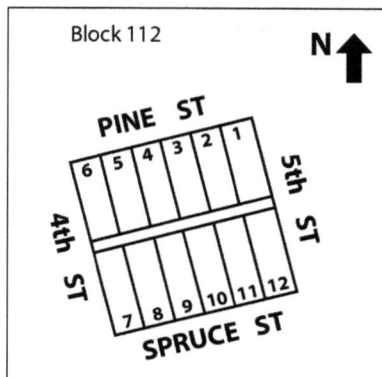

27 Mar 1860, Alfred Miller appoints Horace Annis, Esq attorney to dispose of property on his behalf, witness J W Partridge

20 Apr 1860, Denver City, David Horsefall [Horsfal] assigns 1/4 Interest to Wm Sargent as security for freight and passage to this city from Nebraska City, N.T. Recorded 18 Aug 1860, witnesses H B Harris, E Wier. W B Edson, Recorder

23 Apr 1860, Boulder City Town Company to Nathan & David King, lot 1 block 63, witness M D Cowsert, Secy H C Norton

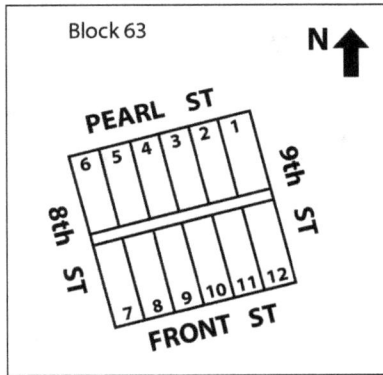

2 May 1860, William K Hughey to James H Russell, Interest No. 34, shares No. 2, 3, and 4

3 May 1860, G W Thorp to John Dale, lot 8 block 119, witness W G Pell, I F Busch, A H Sockman, Agt

3 May 1860, Albert Corbin to Horace Annis, lot 5 block 42, witness A H Lockman, H S Tracy

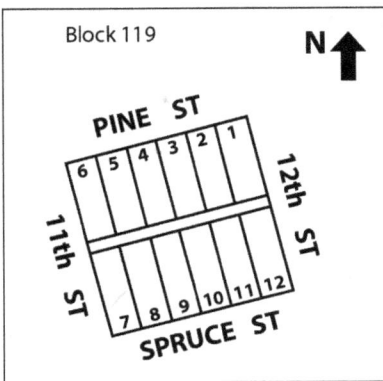

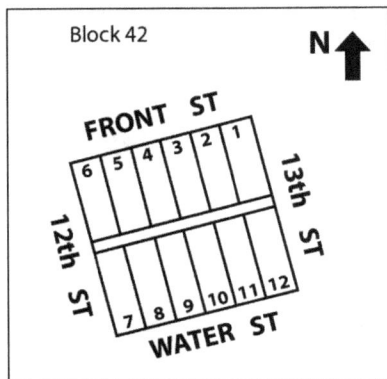

4 June 1860, Boulder City Town Company to F A Squires & Tourtellot, house on lot 7 block 96, director W G Pell, witness M D Cowsert, H C Norton

9 June 1860, William K Hughey to Henry A Newman, 1/60 of his original Interest along with improvements, witness John H Maxon, Notary Public at Nebraska City

9 June 1860, A A Brookfield to Mary Weston, 1/2 house on lot 12 block 120, witness M D Cowsert

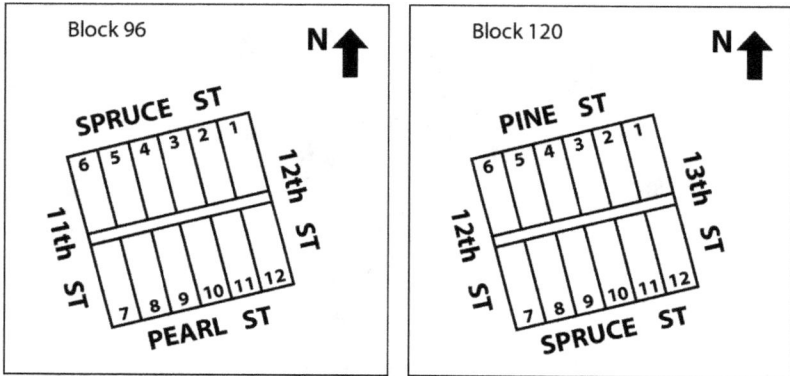

11 June 1860, George Bicknell letter from Elwood, Kansas asking the President of the Boulder City Town Company to have his shares delivered to C E Cook who would settle all tax arrears.

29 June 1860, William M. Scourfield (Arapahoe County, Kansas Territory) to M D Cowsert (Jackson County, Nebraska Territory), house on lot 12 block 95, witness A Jacobs of Arapahoe County, Kansas Territory as notary

30 June 1860, Mark Wittgenstein to W G Pell, lot 8 block 121, witness J H Decker, J B Sheppard

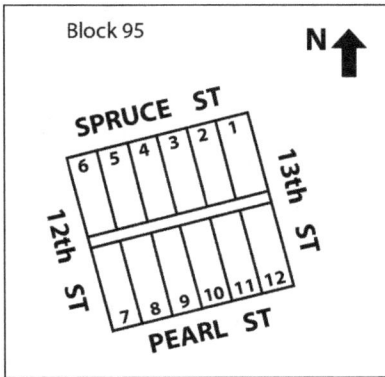

Block 95

SPRUCE ST

6 5 4 3 2 1

12th ST   13th ST

7 8 9 10 11 12

PEARL ST

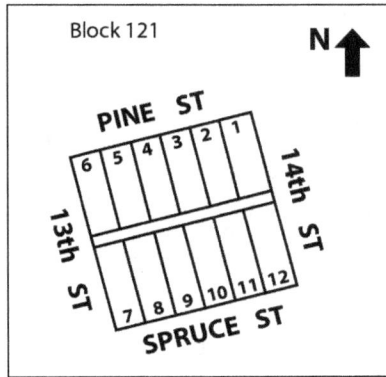

Block 121

PINE ST

6 5 4 3 2 1

13th ST   14th ST

7 8 9 10 11 12

SPRUCE ST

11 July 1860, James H Russell to Henry A Newman, Interest No. 34, shares No. 2, 3 and 4, witnesses J H Decker, H C Norton

19 July 1860, William Mills to B W Perkins and I C Person, house on lot 5 block 67, witnesses Orman E Hobbie, Samuel Wharton

2 Aug 1859 (but probably 1860), David M Wooley as Agent for Louis C Davenport to A Barker, 1/2 Interest No 24, including house, witness M D Cousert, A D Stevens

3 Aug 1860, Horace Annis to W B Edson and W D Edson, lot 4 block 67, witness Peter Collins, Henry Green

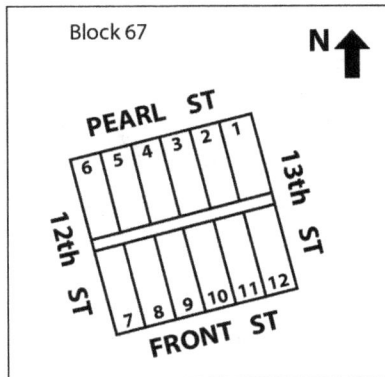

Block 67

PEARL ST

6 5 4 3 2 1

12th ST   13th ST

7 8 9 10 11 12

FRONT ST

6 Aug 1860, W G Pell to A M Buckham, lot 10 block 40; lot 2 block 43

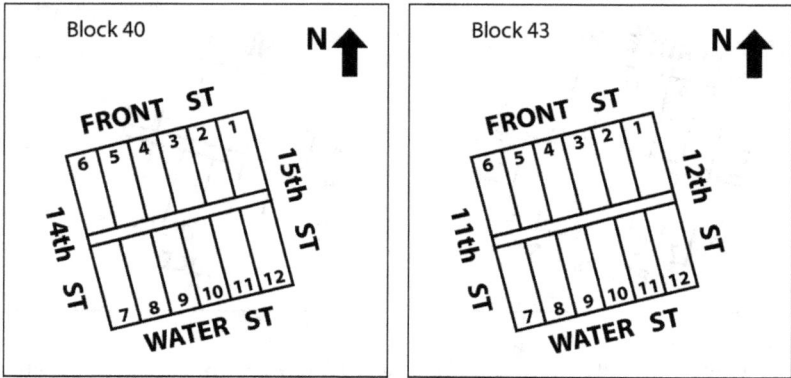

6 Aug 1860, W G Pell to A M Buckham, lot 8 block 121 along with improvements, witness J Whitney, Thos Mosses Jr (Moses ??), W B Edson Recorder for J G Williams Jr

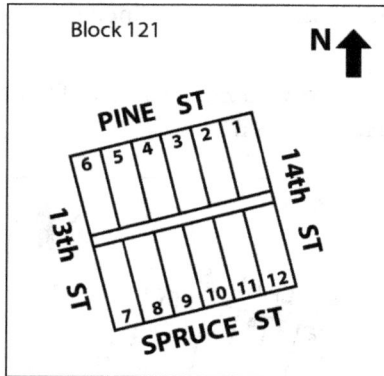

7 Aug 1860, A M Bucham to W B Edson and W S Edson, 1/2 Interest No. 12, lot 2 block 60; lot 6 block 120; lot 9 block 42; lot 2 block 116; lot 7 block 7; lot 8 block 153; lot 1 block 145; lot 3 block 174 along with 1/2 of the unsurveyed portion of Interest No. 12, I Whitney, F A Roberts

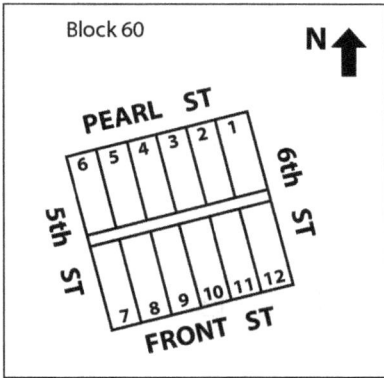

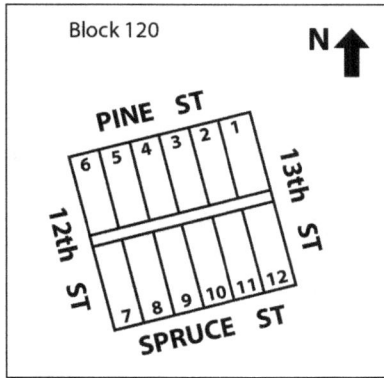

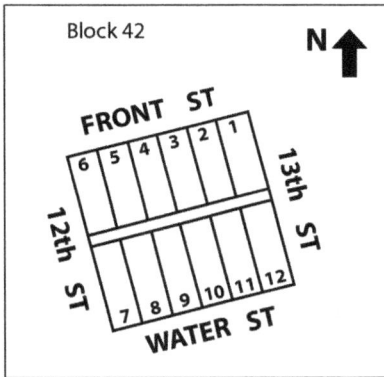

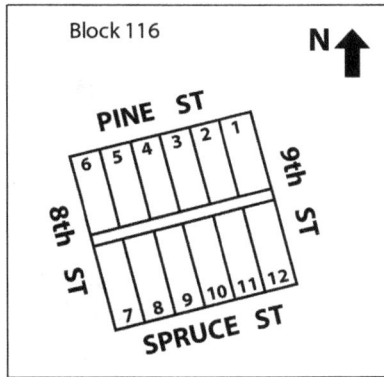

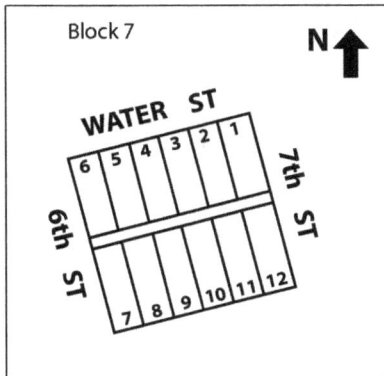

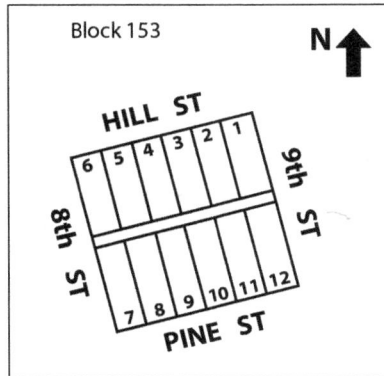

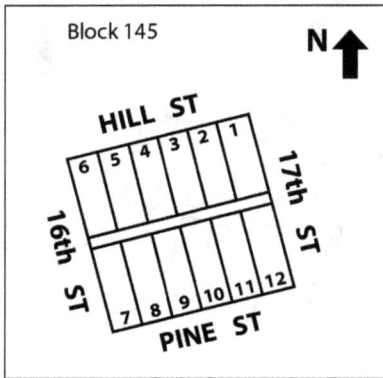

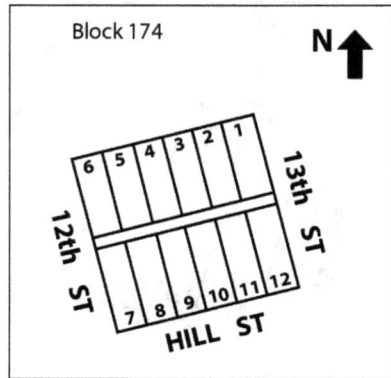

11 Aug 1860, Robert McFarland to (NOT NAMED), Interest No. 40, witnesses J Whitney and C D Davis

14 Aug 1860, J L Boutwell to Jacob Shearer, 1/2 lot 4 block 69, witness W B Edson

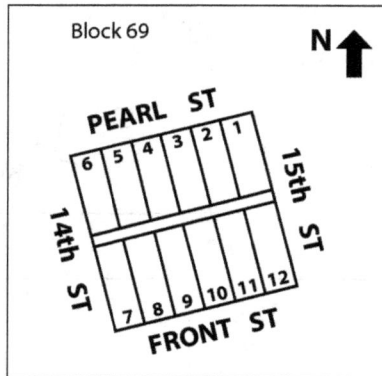

15 Aug 1860, R L Simpson to H O Griggs, lot 12 block 13; lot 11 block 172 in Interest No. 46, witnesses G W Coffin, J R Tryon

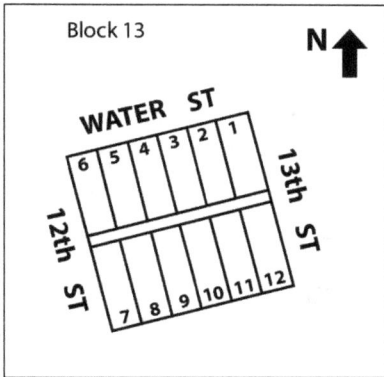

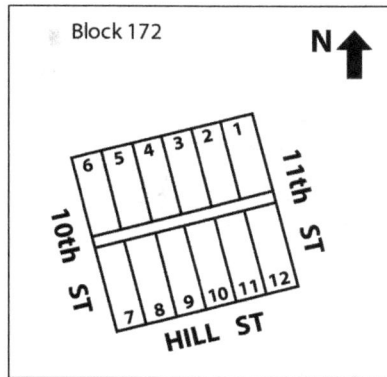

18 Aug 1860, David Parlin to Horace Annis, lot 12 block 68; lot 3 block 100, witness A Mert, W B Edson, Recorder

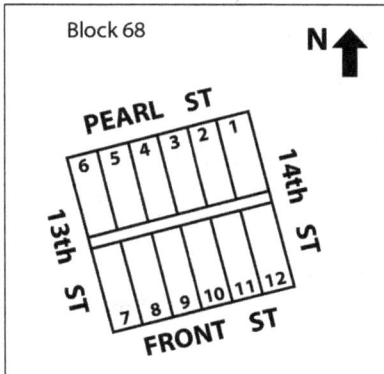

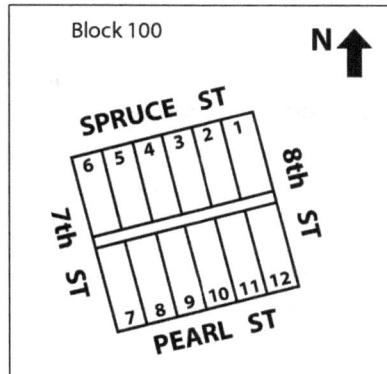

20 Aug 1860, C J Goss, Pell & Lowe to Daniel Pound, lot 11 block 95 except the Indian claim, witnesses W B Edson

20 Aug 1860, Owen Linderman to Horace Tarbox, lot 5 block 96, witnesses Jno L Buell, M W Towner

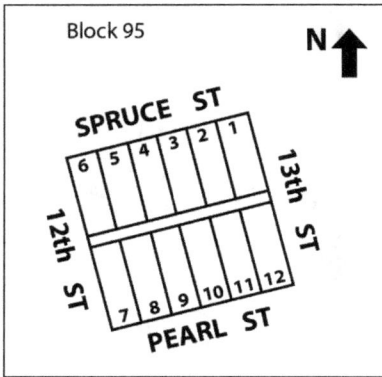

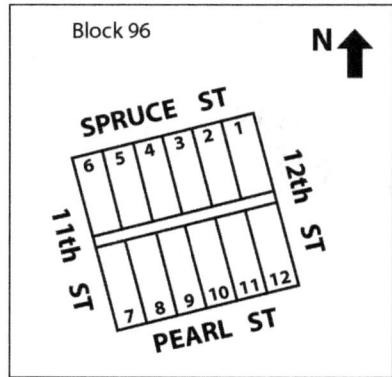

31 Aug 1860, received of G W Nichols, $2 to apply on shares No. 1 and 2 in the above interest for taxes on the Gregory Road. W B Edson, Treasurer

31 Aug 1860, received of G W Nichols, $2 on shares No. 1 and 2 in the above interest for taxes on Gregory Road. W B Edson, Treasurer.

31 Aug 1860, received of G W Nichols, $2 to apply to share No. 1 and 2 about interest for road taxes to Gregory. W B Edson, Treasurer

1 Sept 1860, Charles E Cook, agent for George Bicknell to Joab Enoz [Enos], lot 4 block 94 with the buildings, witnesses Thomas Akins, A M Buckham

11 Sept 1860, J Whitney to W B Edson and J G Williams, lot 2 block 65 along with his interests in lots of lumber at Partridge shingle mill and Tarbox & Donnelly's saw mill, witness P G Cooper

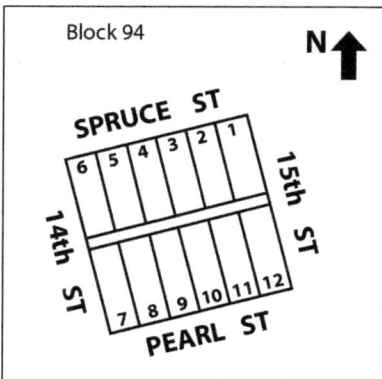

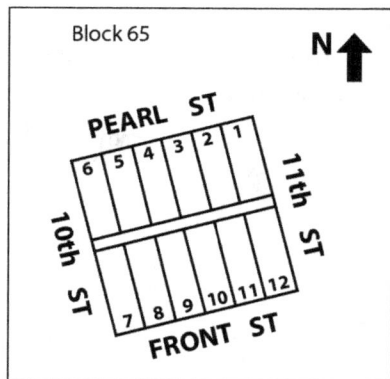

21 Sept 1860, Daniel B Williams to Daniel Pound, lot 2 block 67 except the Indian claim, witness John Southworth

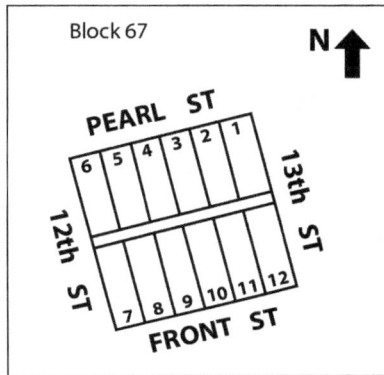

22 Sept 1860, Henderson interest forfeited to the Boulder City Town Company

block	lot	block	lot	block	lot	block	lot
69	12	65	8	103	11	63	8
103	12	158	12	158	6	98	2
152	2	98	1	39	4	16	5
168	12	48	2	166	5	178	1
106	3	(only 17 lots listed)					

3 Oct 1860, Boulder City Town Company to James B Ross Interest No. 58, Share No. 1
3 Oct 1860, Boulder City Town Company to James B Ross Interest No. 58, Share No. 2
3 Oct 1860, Boulder City Town Company to James B Ross Interest No. 58, Share No. 3
3 Oct 1860, Boulder City Town Company to James B Ross Interest No. 58, Share No. 4

4 Oct 1860, M W Towner to Joseph H Jamison, lot 5 block 68 along with improvements, witness W S Howard, C D Davis

4 Oct 1860, James R Parker to M W Towner, lot 6 block 66 with improvements, witness C D Davis, W G Howard

Block 68 — PEARL ST, 6 5 4 3 2 1, 13th ST, 14th ST, 7 8 9 10 11 12, FRONT ST

Block 66 — PEARL ST, 6 5 4 3 2 1, 11th ST, 12th ST, 7 8 9 10 11 12, FRONT ST

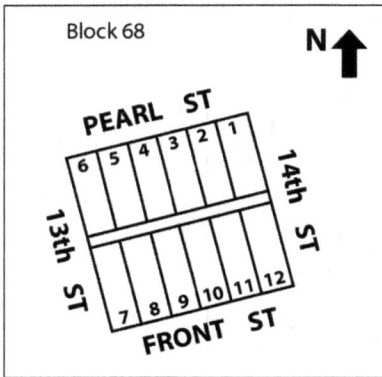

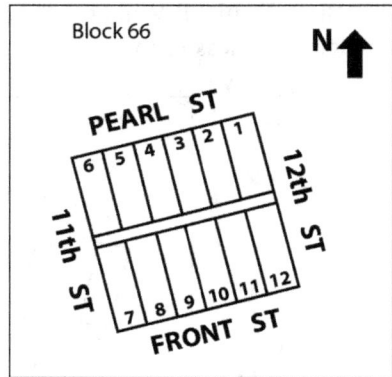

10 Oct 1860, M W Towner to J W Partridge, lot 7 block 47, witness C D Davis, A Miller

24 Oct 1860, James W Partridge to Alfred Miller, lot 7 block 47, shingle machine, drag saw and torts, witness J A Tourtellot

3 Nov 1860, H Annis to H C Shrader, lot 1 block 68, witness D H Nichols, A H Grovenor

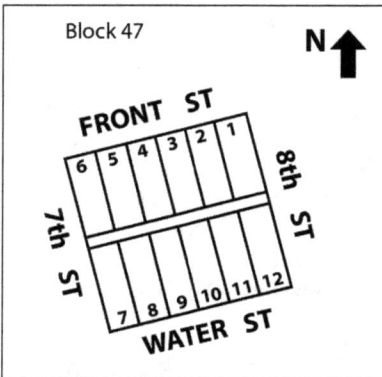

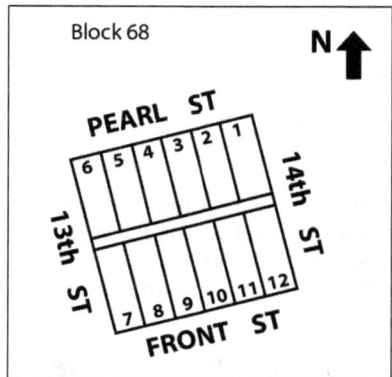

Block 47 — FRONT ST, 6 5 4 3 2 1, 7th ST, 8th ST, 7 8 9 10 11 12, WATER ST

Block 68 — PEARL ST, 6 5 4 3 2 1, 13th ST, 14th ST, 7 8 9 10 11 12, FRONT ST

8 Nov 1860, L L Locklin to Robert E Stackhouse, lot 5 block 16; lot 11 block 13; lot 12 block 168; lot 5 block 166; 1/2 lot 3 block 6, witness J G Williams, Jr

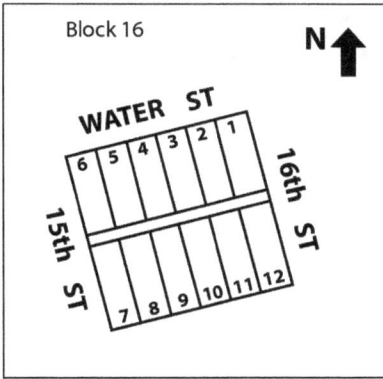

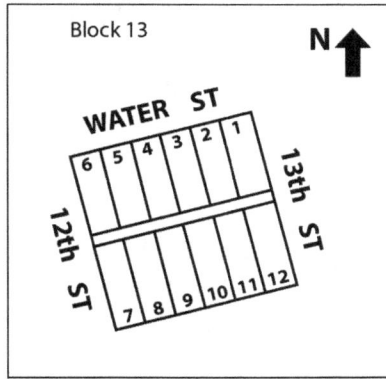

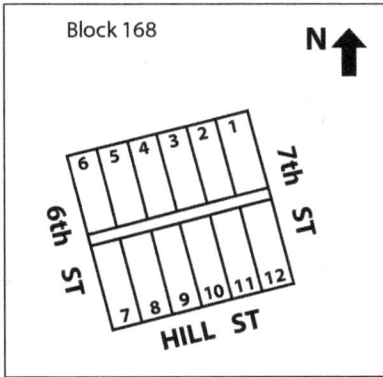

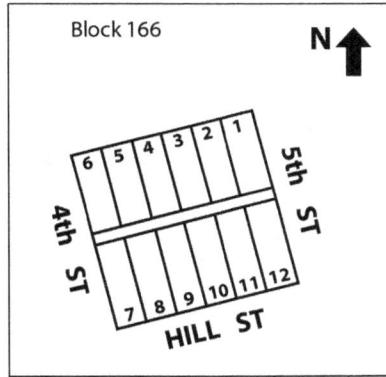

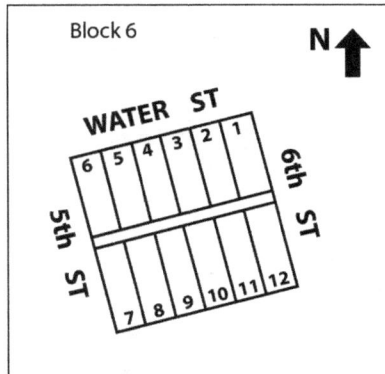

9 Nov 1860, A A Brookfield to L L Locklin, lot 12 block 69; lot 11 block 103; lot 1 block 178; lot 12 block 122; lot 6 block 158; lot 5 block 16; lot 12 block 168; lot 5 block 166; 1/2 block 3 block 6, witness J G Williams, Jr

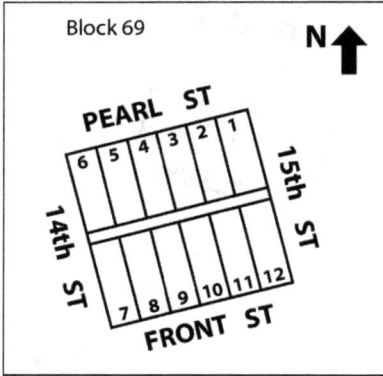

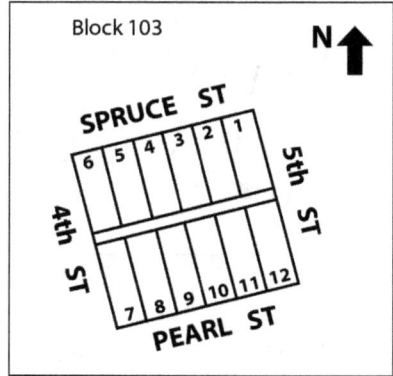

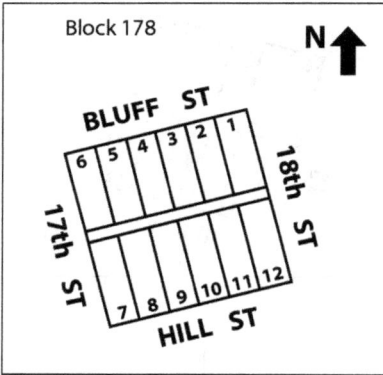

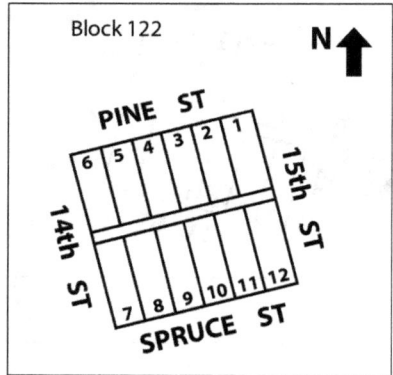

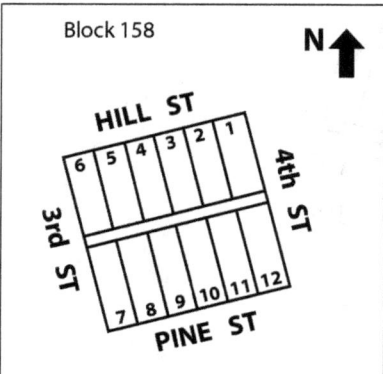

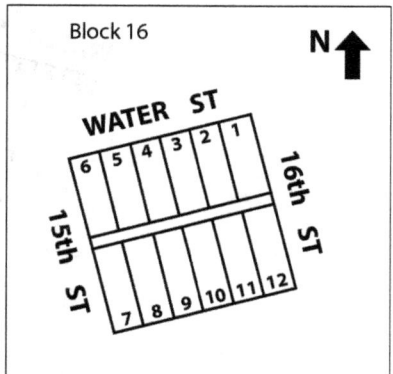

Block 166

Block 6

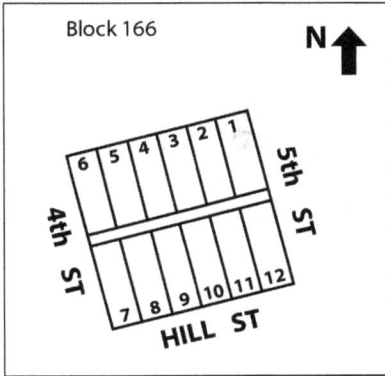

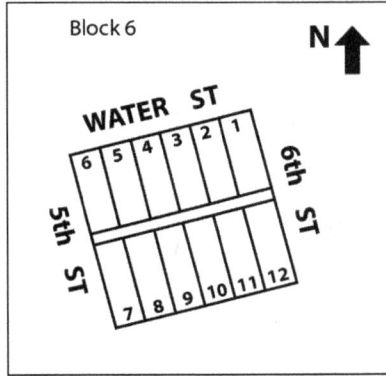

9 Nov 1860, L L Locklin to A A Brookfield, lot 8 block 65; lot 8 block 63; lot 12 block 103; lot 2 block 98; lot 2 block 152; lot 1 block 98; lot 4 block 39; lot 2 block 48; lot 4 block 67; 1/2 lot 3 block 6, J G Williams, Jr

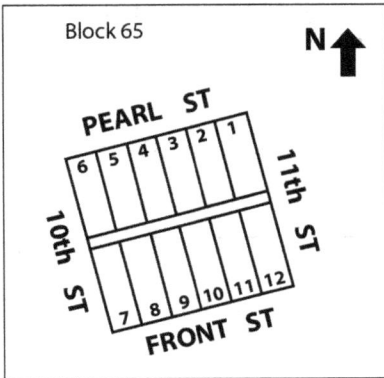

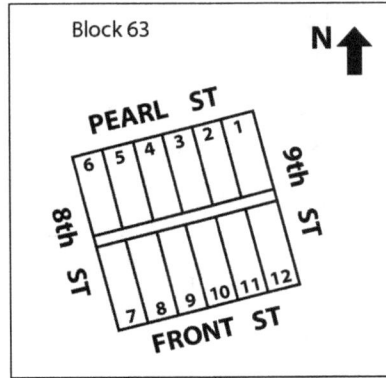

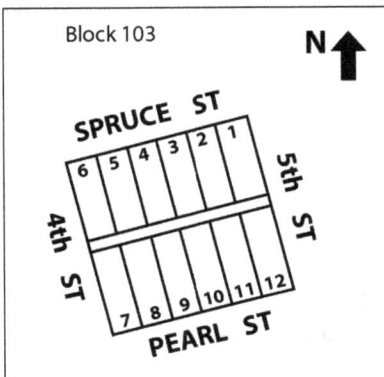

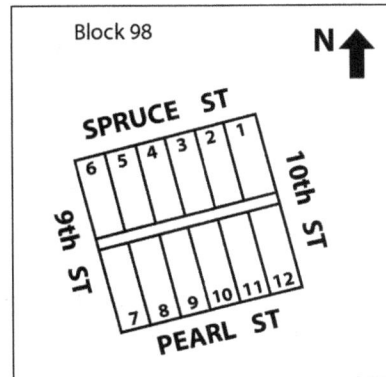

Block 65

Block 63

Block 103

Block 98

Block 152

HILL ST
6 5 4 3 2 1
9th ST
10th ST
7 8 9 10 11 12
PINE ST

Block 51

FRONT ST
6 5 4 3 2 1
3rd ST
4th ST
7 8 9 10 11 12
WATER ST

Block 48

FRONT ST
6 5 4 3 2 1
6th ST
7th ST
7 8 9 10 11 12
WATER ST

Block 67

PEARL ST
6 5 4 3 2 1
12th ST
13th ST
7 8 9 10 11 12
FRONT ST

Block 6

WATER ST
6 5 4 3 2 1
5th ST
6th ST
7 8 9 10 11 12

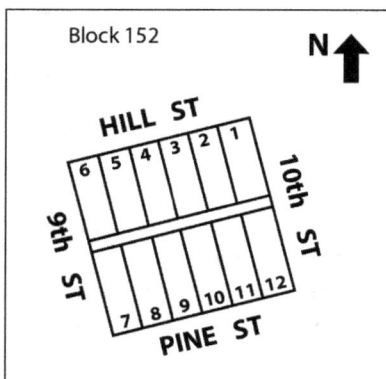

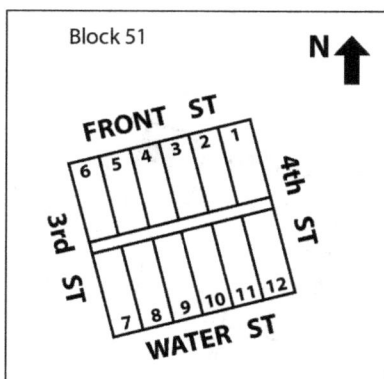

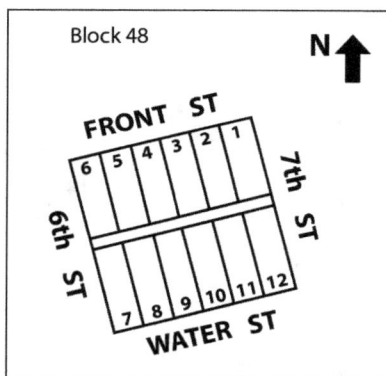

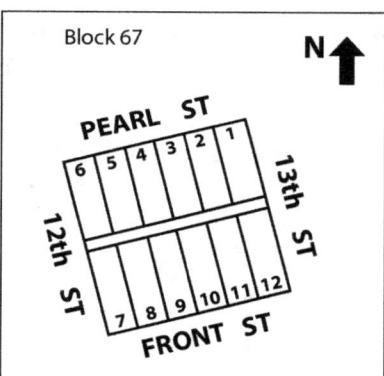

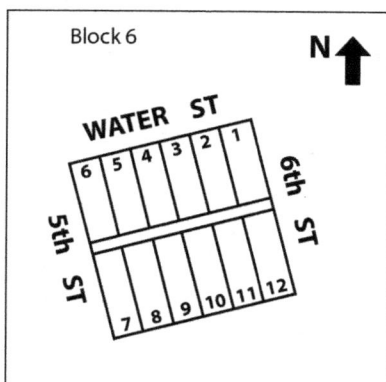

9 Nov 1860, A M Buckham to T J Jones, lot 8 block 121, the lot was given to A M Buckham by W G Pell on 6 Aug 1860, witness J G Williams, Jr

9 Nov 1860, A M Buckham to T J Jones, lot 1 block 67, J G Williams, Jr

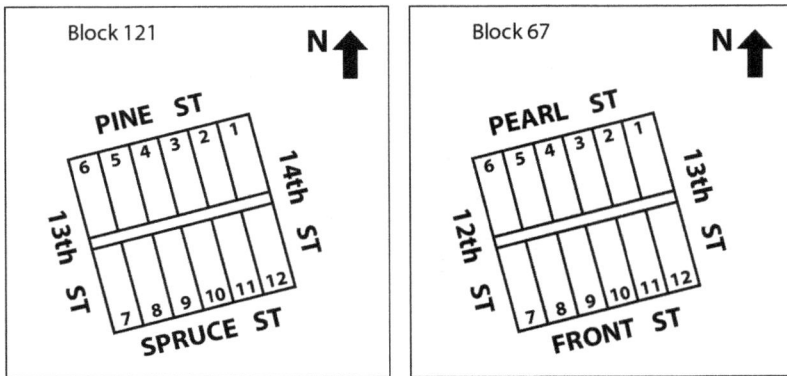

27 Nov 1860, J W Partridge to Hanford Reed of Denver City, lot 7 block 47 with the shingle mill machine and machinery, witness Warren, J M Martin

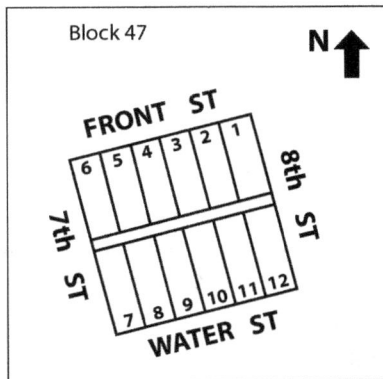

4 Dec 1860, Albert Corbin to William Ails, Interest No. 25

block	lot	block	lot	block	lot	block	lot
118	12	64	9	44	4	59	6
120	4	43	10	114	7	113	2
112	5	111	1	46	5	47	4
151	1	145	5	173	10	11	12
176	3						

witnesses J G Williams, Jr, J V Gibbons

13 Dec 1860, Samuel E Stephenson to C H Gardner, house on lot 11 block 96, witness Jacob P Kinsey

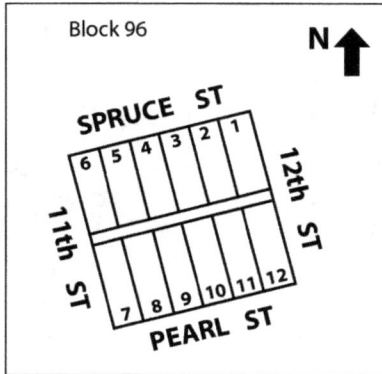

15 Dec 1860, T J Jones to George Mack, 1/4 Interest No. 39, witness J G Williams, Jr

1861

22 Jan 1861, (crossed out) L L Locklin to James Whittier of Golden City public land containing 160 acres, Jackson County, Jefferson Territory, known as Locklin's claim on Boulder Creek, about 6 miles North and East of Boulder City, on the west by Barney's Claim, on the east by Harris's claim, with the improvement, G W Nichols, County Recorder

23 Jan 1861, James W Partridge and Ivey Partridge to John H Martin of Denver City, house on lot 6 block 41, witness E G Tompkins, H Reed

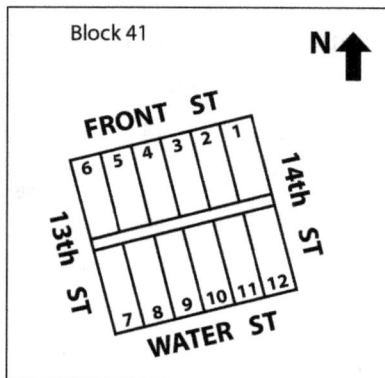

29 Jan 1861, Jacob P Kinsey to Freeman Belcher, Interest No. 30, share No. 3, witness T Robinson

29 Jan 1861, Jacob P Kinsey to Chas H Gardner, house on lot 11 block 16, witness James G Robinson

8 Feb 1861, Leonidas Mitchel and wife Hattie J Mitchel convey to Sylvester Hill, house on block 95, lot 8, witness J L McCormick

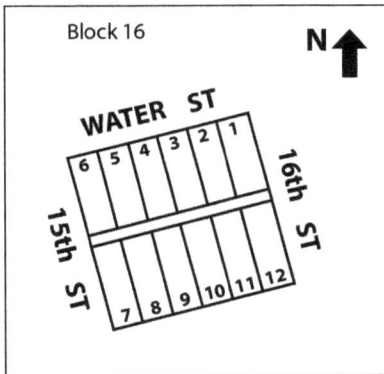

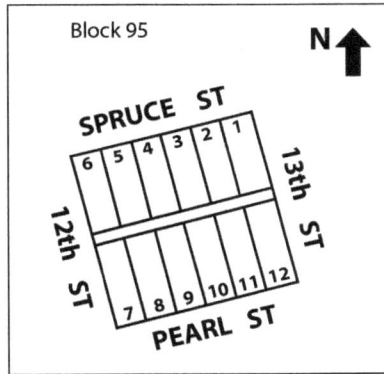

13 Feb 1861, Sheriffs Sale by John R Edick, Sheriff of Jackson County, Territory of Jefferson, sold to Joab & Cyrus H Enos all of title and interest of Albert Corbin and David S Corbin, block 157, lot 1, block 153, lot 4, block 148, lot 9, block 119, lot 12. These lots were sold at public auction to satisfy judgment in favor of J H Decker and H Annis against Albert and David S Corbin. Witness David Parlin

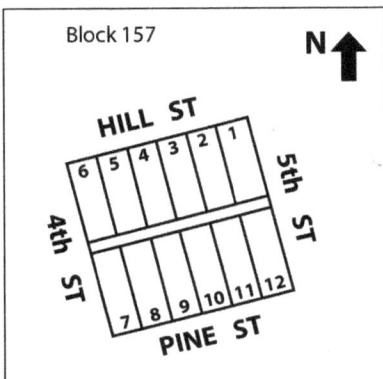

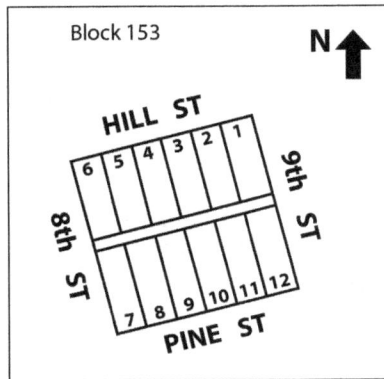

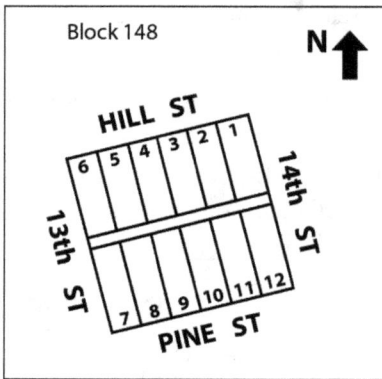

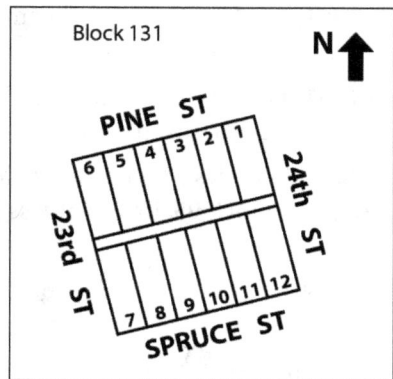

21 Feb 1861, Daniel W Buel [Buell] to Tourtellot & Squires, Interest No. 58, witness J H Decker

6 Mar 1861, A A Brookfield to Wm M Skiner [Skinner], lot 10 block 66, witness J G Williams, Jr, J H Decker

12 Mar 1861, M D Cowsert to Daniel Pound, lot 12 block 95, witness O P Goodwin, Geo W Nichols

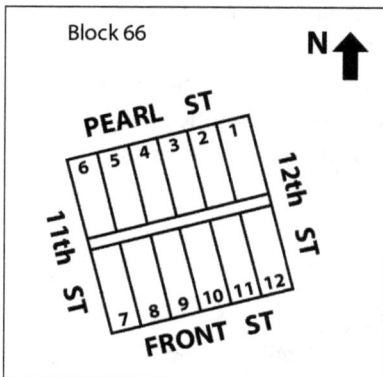

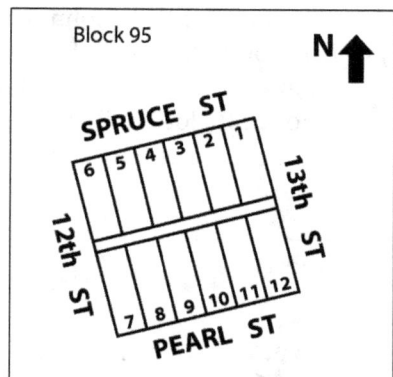

12 Mar 1861, George Allee to Edward Donnelly and Horace Tarbox, lot 7 block 119; lot 12 block 12, witnesses E J Henderson, John R Esbeck

Block 119 — N

PINE ST
6 5 4 3 2 1
11th ST | 12th ST
7 8 9 10 11 12
SPRUCE ST

Block 12 — N

WATER ST
6 5 4 3 2 1
11th ST | 12th ST
7 8 9 10 11 12

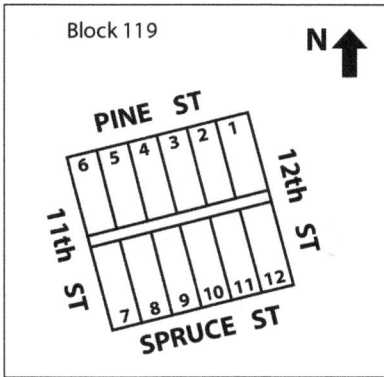

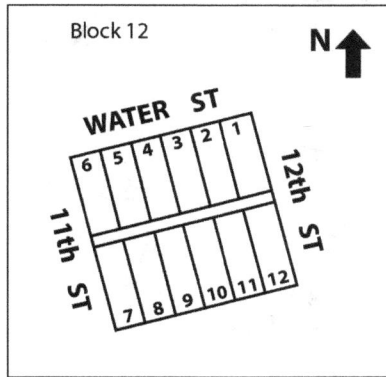

12 Mar 1861, George Briggs by J H Decker, Agent to W H Millard & T A Griffith, lot 6 block 67, witness J G Williams, Jr

12 Mar 1861, Horace Annis to A Barker, lot 1 block 42, witness Warren, Allen

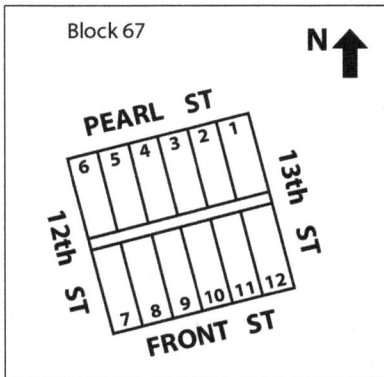

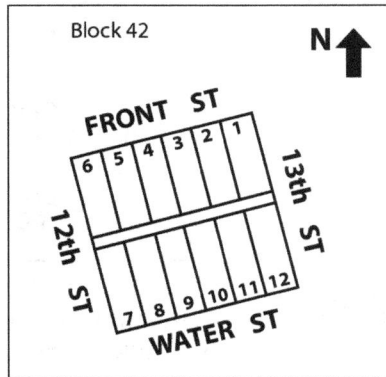

Block 67 — N

PEARL ST
6 5 4 3 2 1
12th ST | 13th ST
7 8 9 10 11 12
FRONT ST

Block 42 — N

FRONT ST
6 5 4 3 2 1
12th ST | 13th ST
7 8 9 10 11 12
WATER ST

12 Mar 1861, George W Thorp to Edward Donnelly and Horace Tarbox, lot 3 block 65, witness J A Tourtellot

16 Mar 1861, George W Thorp to David M Parlin, lot 10 block 92, witness C M Clouser

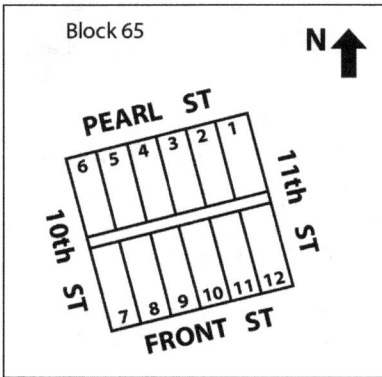

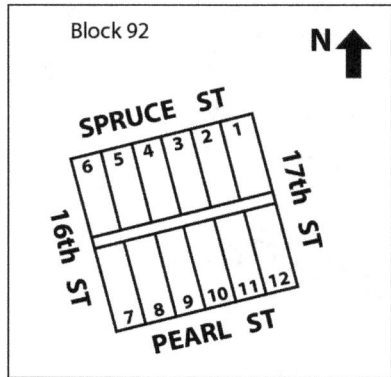

18 Mar 1861, H P Butler to C H Gardner, lot above lot 11, block 96

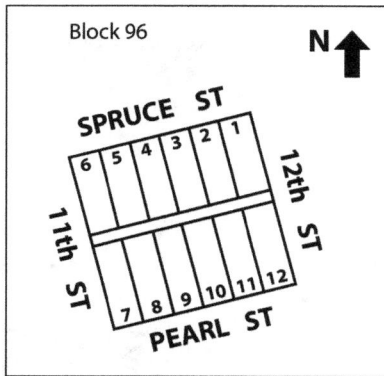

20 Mar 1861, A W Harris to Freeman Belcher & Jacob P Kinsey, lot 3 block 104; lot 12 block 152; lot 4 block 70; lot 4 block 58; lot 9 block 50, witness H C Norton

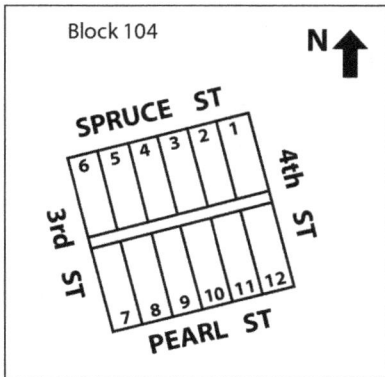

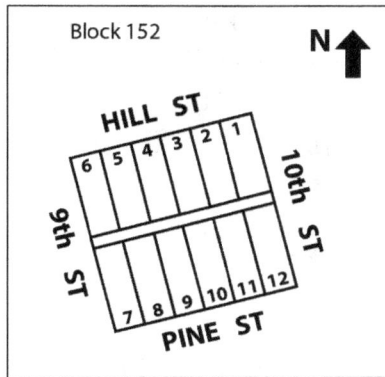

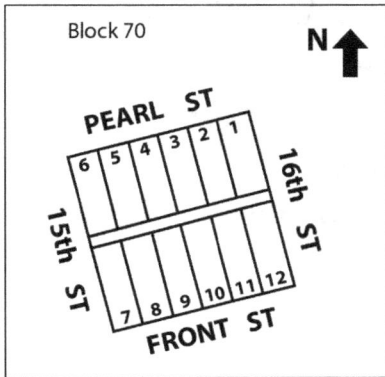

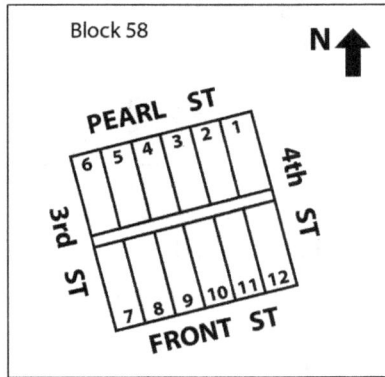

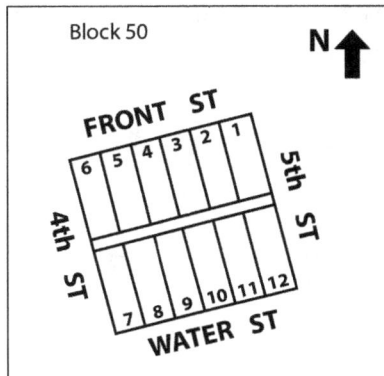

11 Apr 1861, J R Palmer & Co to M L Locklin, one white horse, witness T H Welch, signed J R Palmer, W H E Smith, Recorder G W Nichols

14 Apr 1861, Wm Street to Clark Bryant, lot 3 block 67, witness Kate Elsey

15 April 1861, Charles M Clouser to David Parlin, 50'x50' of lot 10 block 95, witnesses J H Decker, J H Greenley [Greenly], H Annis

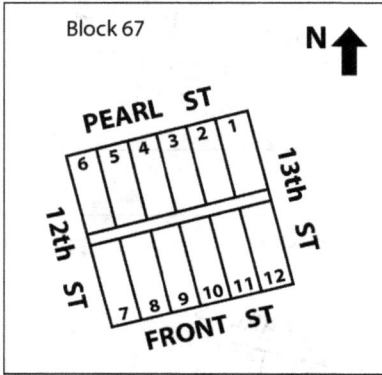

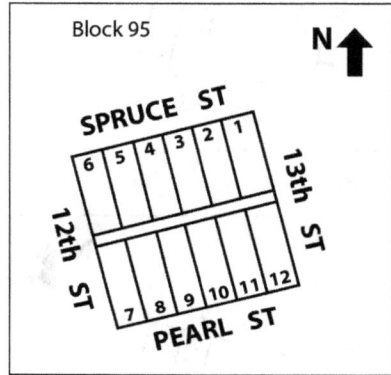

15 April 1861, George Mack to M W Towner, Interest No. 39, witness Lenffrett [Lafayette] Akins

23 Apr 1861, L L Locklin to George W Thorpe, one horse, signed L L Locklin, M L Locklin

6 June 1861, J H Jamison to A J Maxwell, lot 5, block 68, witness Lafayette Akins

10 June 1861, George W Thorpe to Thomas Akins, house on lot 5 block 95, lot 7 in Boulder City (no block number listed), witness Wm Vanderhuff

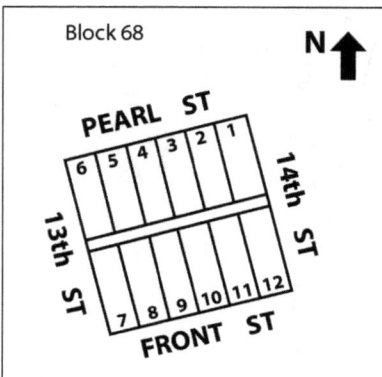

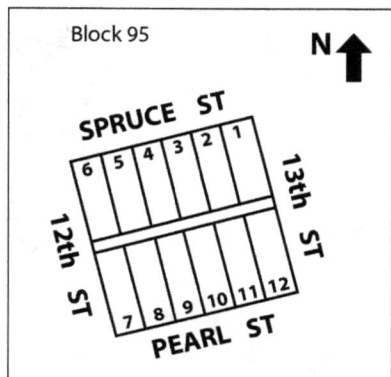

11 June 1861, J D Scott to A J Macky and Hiram Buck, one black cow, witness J D Sutphen

12 June 1861, J D Scott to P M Housel of Gold Hill, one muley cow red and one bindle cow 4 years old, one black cow about 8 years old, one thirly horse black, witness M D Cowsert

31 June 1861, J Whitney to Robert E Stackhouse, lot 8 block 92, witness J Smith

6 July 1861, John H Martin of Denver City to G W Horton, quit claim deed 75 square of shingles at Boulder City, lot 6 block 41, witnesses G W Perkins, H Annis

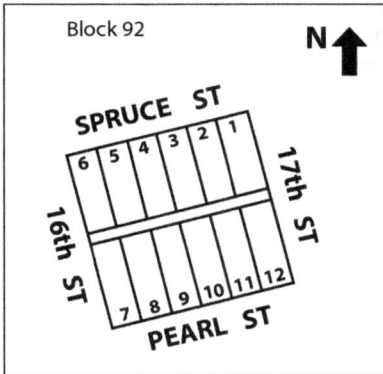

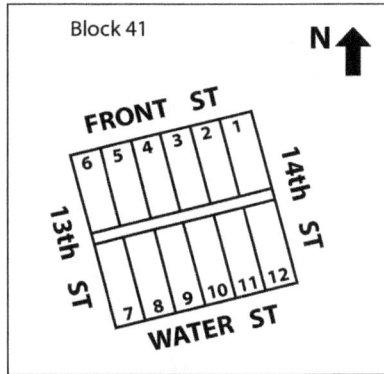

8 July 1861, E S Warren to J R Parker, one original Interest No. 55 except two lots sold before this date, witness M W Towner, V D Parker

11 July 1861, Alfred Miller by H Annis his attorney to Hanford Reed, lot 7 block 47 and shingle machine, witnesses C J Goss, J G Williams, Jr

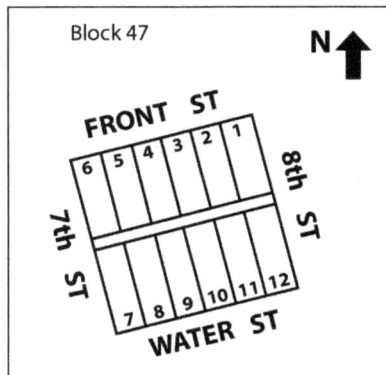

13 July 1861, Hanford Reed of Denver to George W Horton of Boulder City, shingle mill tools and machinery and land described in a deed to me by J W Partridge in the winter of 1860 on file with the Recorders office in Boulder City or village, witnesses G Squires, William Spartings

16 July 1861, John H Martin to George W Horton the deed made to John H Martin by J W Partridge, 1/2 interest in the shingle machinery and fixtures, witnesses G W Perkins, H Annis

16 July 1861, Jas W Partridge and George W Horton to J H Martin of Denver City, 1/2 interest in shingle mill machinery formerly built and owned by J W Partridge, witness G W Perkins, Hanford Reed

16 July 1861, J W Partridge and Hanford Reed of Denver City by J H Martin to J A Martin, 1/2 interest in a shingle mill formerly built and owned by J W Partridge in Boulder, witness Geo W Perkins, H Annis

18 July 1861, James R Parker to Joab and Cyrus H Enos, one original Interest No. 55, except 2 lots previously sold, witnesses V D Parker, H C Houley

17 Aug 1861, David Parlin to A J Macky, 50'x50' lot 10 block 95, J G Williams, Jr, D H Nichols

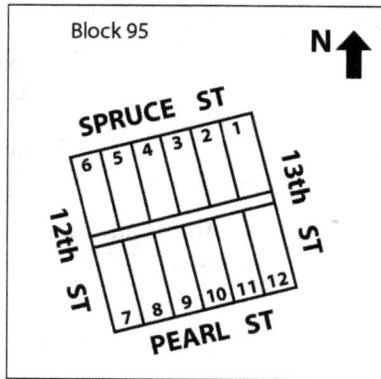

3 Sept 1861, J H Martin of Denver City to G W Horton, 1/2 interest in a shingle mill and machinery formerly built and owned by J W Partridge, witnesses at Denver City, W D Davis, Jno W Todd

14 Sept 1861, J H Martin of Denver City to H Reed, 1/2 interest in a shingle mill and machinery formerly built and owned by J W Partridge, witnesses at Denver City T W Smith, J E Weld

25 Nov 1861, George H Horton to Hanford Reed of Denver, 1/2 interest in a shingle mill and machinery, witness J W Partridge

19 Dec 1861, A J Macky to David Parlin (paid by Hiram Buck), 1/2 of (front) 50' of lot 10, block 95 with buildings, witnesses J [G]Williams Jr, David H Nichols, A Barker Recorder, recorded on Vol A p. 93 [ill. facing page]

1862

19 Mar 1862, Charles M Clouser to Matilda Parlin, west 90' of lot 10, block 95, witness David Parlin [ill. facing page]

2 June 1862, Joab Enos, Cyrus H Enos assigned to David Pound, all of right, title and interests. Witnesses J G Williams Jr, Jonathan Wells Jr, recorded by D Pound on **3 Mar 1863**; block 157, lot 1; block 153, lot 4; block 148, lot 9; block 119, lot 6; plus lots conveyed to Joab Enos and Cyrus H Enos from J R Parker on **19 July 1861** in interest no 55 except 2 lots sold by the original owner; also block 94, lot 4. David Parlin, Justice of the Peace

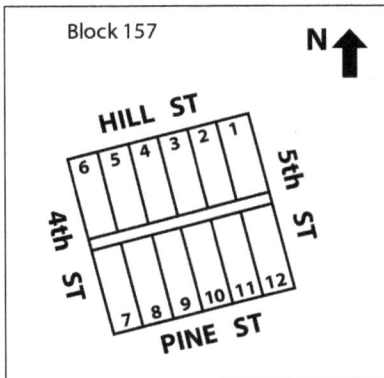

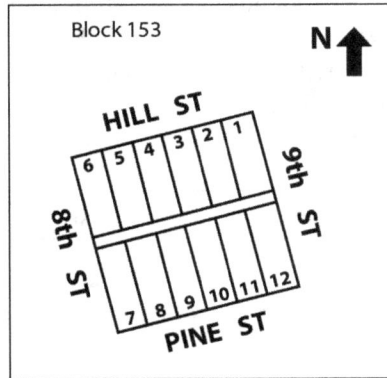

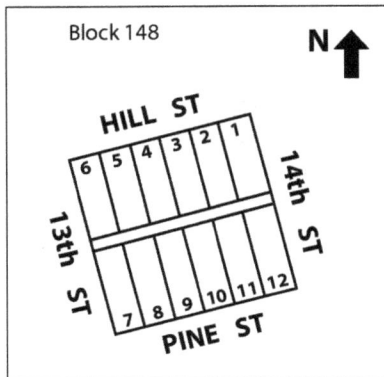

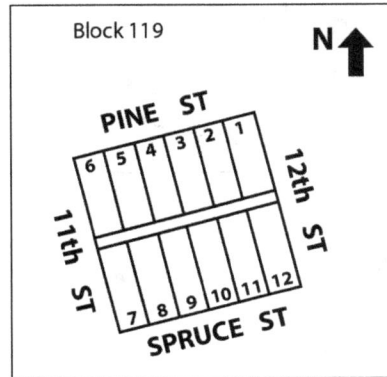

3 June 1862, A A Brookfield conveys to M W Towner, block 95, lot 3 (side note says that the correct lot number is 5)

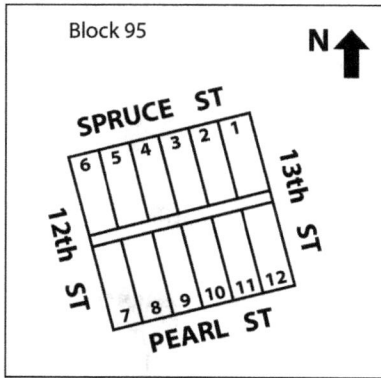

5 June 1862, Albert and David S Corbin to Daniel Pound, lot 1 block 157, lot 4 block 153, lot 9 block 148, lot 6 block 119 as described in a deed from John R Edick dated 13 Feb 1861, sold to satisfy a judgment against Albert and David S Corbin by the said John R Edick, Sheriff of Jackson County, Jefferson Territory, all the lots in Interest No. 55 except 2 lots said to have been sold by the original owner, as designated in a deed from J R Parker dated 19 July 1861, and lot 4 block 94, witness Joab Enos, Cyrus H Enos

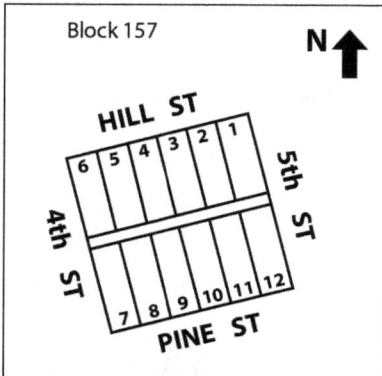

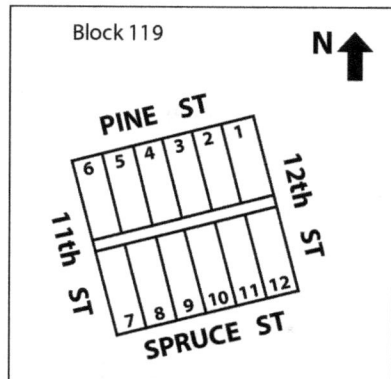

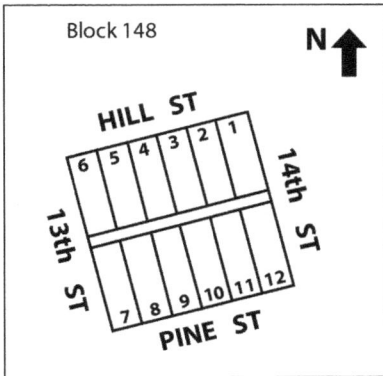

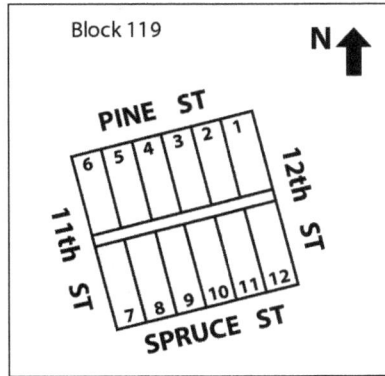

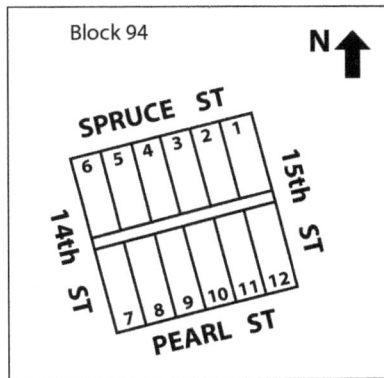

1863

3 Mar 1863, Daniel Pound to Charles W Smith block 94, lot 4. witness A J Macky, JP [ill. above]

15 March 1863, A A Brookfield conveys to Daniel Pound, block 95, lot 3, witness A J Macky [ill. facing page]

15 or 16 March 1863 (no date but between two items with those dates), CROSSED OUT, M W Towner, house and lot (no numbers) to C B Gillett

16 Mar 1863, A A Brookfield appeared before A J Macky, J P to affirm his signature on the above deed

21 May 1863, Share no. 1, Interest No. 30 from A W Harris to G W Horton, except 2 lots—one sold to J L Scherrer, the other to Albert Cushman

1 Sept 1863, P G Cooper of Washington County, Nebraska Territory by agent Daniel Pound to Sylvester Hill, block 95, lot 9, in the original interest of Mr Bull [Buell]

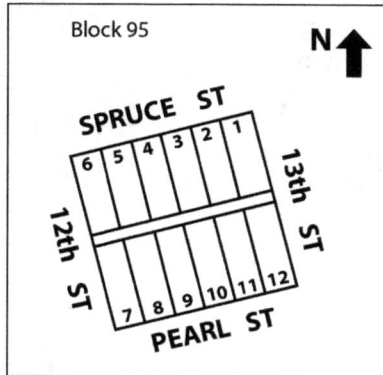

1864

9 Apr 1864, Wm Barney to Daniel Pound, witness G W Nichols

block	lot	block	lot	block	lot	block	lot
67	6	67	9	98	7	150	11
38	6	49	9	93	9	62	6
150	10	154	1	147	8	176	7
167	8	167	5	103	3	156	3
39	10						

24 July 1864, Sylvester Hill to Daniel Pound, block 67, lot 1, witnesses A J Mackey [Macky], J E Duhnis

27 July 1864, C W Smith to Daniel Pound (no block or lot listed)

7 Aug 1864, Sylvester Hill to Daniel Pound, block 68, lot 6, witness Geo Emit Werner, Wm Pound

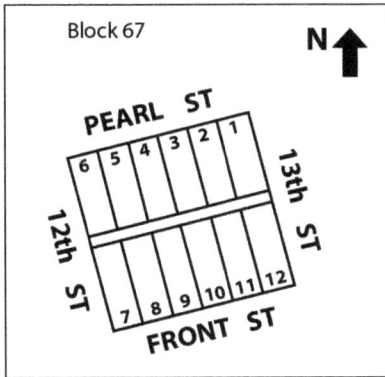

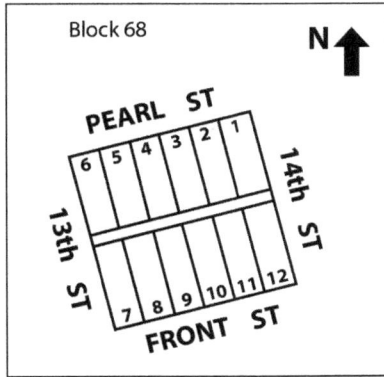

8 Sept 1864, D H Nichols, agent for Horace Annis to Daniel Pound, block 68, lot 1; block 68, lot 12; block 42, lot 5

14 Sept 1864, Marquis W Towner to Daniel Pound, block 42, lot 4; block 42, lot 8; block 14, lot 5, witness Robert McFarland, Wm Pound

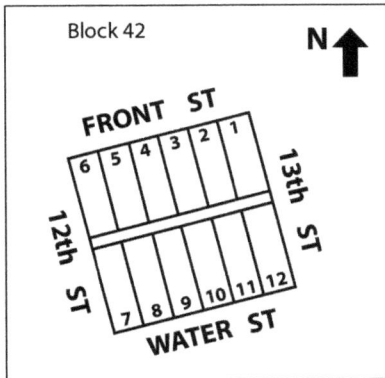

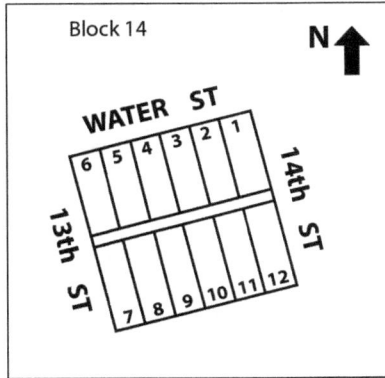

Transfer List

(no dates)

block 7, lot 6	M W Towner
block 9, lot 12	Jno L Buell, Goss, Pell & Lowe
block 10, lot 12	Charles B Aikens [Akins]
block 12, lot 4	Hunt & Appleton
block 12, lot 5	A E Baugh
block 12, lot 7	A E Baugh
block 13, lot 7	Charles B Aikens [Akins]
block 14, lot 5	George Hackleman to M W Towner
block 14, lot 9	Robert McFarland
block 14, lot 10	P G Cooper
Block 15, lot 8	A W Harris
Block 16, lot 2	A M Hunt
Block 17, lot 2	A W Harris
Block 17, lot 7	Jno L Buell, Goss Pell & Lowe
Block 38, lot 9	A M Hunt
Block 39, lot 6	A W Harris
Block 40, lot 1	P G Cooper
Block 40, lot 6	Geo Hackelman, A M W Towner
Block 40, lot 11	Geo Hackleman, A M W Towner
Block 41, lot 9	Daniel Williams
block 42, lot 4	T J Jones, M W Towner
block 42, lot 8	M W Towner
Block 43, lot 3	Daniel Williams
Block 43, lot 5	Hunt & Appleton
Block 43, lot 9	A E Baugh
Block 43, lot 12	Geo Hackleman, A M W Towner
Block 44, lot 1	Chas B Aikens [Akins]
Block 44, lot 5	A E Baugh
Block 44, lot 6	E Donnelly
Block 44, lot 10	M W Towner
Block 45, lot 4	Jno L Buell, Goss Pell & Lowe
Block 45, lot 11	Jno L Buell, Goss Pell & Lowe

Block 45, lot 12	A E Baugh
Block 46, lot 7	Daniel Williams
Block 46, lot 11	Chas B Aikens [Akins]
Block 47, lot 5	A E Baugh
Block 47, lot 7	M W Towner
Block 50, lot 1	Geo Hackleman, A M W Towner
Block 50, lot 5	P G Cooper
Block 50, lot 9	A W Harris
Block 51, lot 6	Robert McFarland
Block 51, lot 10	A M Hunt
Block 51, lot 11	Robert McFarland
Block 51, lot 12	P G Cooper
Block 58, lot 4	A W Harris
Block 58, lot 10	Daniel Williams
Block 58, lot 12	A W Harris (crossed out)
Block 59, lot 1	A E Baugh
Block 59, lot 4	Daniel Williams
Block 60, lot 3	M W Towner
Block 60, lot 6	The Aikins [Akins]
Block 60, lot 7	Chas B Aikens [Akins]
Block 60, lot 9	Robert McFarland
Block 61, lot 1	Jno L Buell, Goss, Pell & Lowe
Block 61, lot 4	G Hackelman, A M W Towner
Block 61, lot 7	P G Cooper
Block 62, lot 3	A W Harris
Block 63, lot 1	Town Company to N & D King
Block 63, lot 4	G Hackelman, A M W Towner
Block 63, lot 7	A M Hunt
Block 64, lot 3	E Donnelly
Block 64, lot 4	Chas B Aikens [Akins]
Block 64, lot 7	A E Baugh
Block 64, lot 12	Daniel Williams
Block 65, lot 4	P G Cooper
Block 65, lot 5	Robert McFarland

Block 65, lot 10	A M Hunt
Block 66, lot 4	Daniel Blocher, B A Sinn
Block 66, lot 7	A W Harris
Block 67, lot 2	Daniel Williams, A Daniel Pound
Block 68, lot 5	M W Towner, J M Jemison [Jamison], J Maxwell
Block 68, lot 6	M W Towner
Block 69, lot 6	M W Towner
Block 70, lot 4	A W Harris
Block 70, lot 8	Robert McFarland
Block 71, lot 1	Robert McFarland
Block 71, lot 2	Geo Hackelman, A M W Towner
Block 71, lot 9	Robert McFarland
Block 71, lot 10	P G Cooper
Block 71, lot 12	P G Cooper
Block 93, lot 6	M W Towner
Block 94, lot 3	Jno L Buell, Goss, Pell & Lowe
Block 94, lot 10	Robert McFarland
Block 94, lot 12	N Connelly, S W Tower
Block 95, lot 8	Leonidas Mitchel, Sylvester Hill
Block 95, lot 9	P G Cooper
Block 95, lot 11	Jno L Buell, Goss, Pell & Lowe, D Pound
Block 96, lot 9	Geo Hackelman, M W Towner
Block 96, lot 10	Jno L Buell, Crow and Brundy
Block 96, lot 12	T J Jones
Block 97, lot 11	Tarbox & Donnelly, donated from Town Co
Block 97, lot 12	Tarbox & Donnelly, donated from Town Co
Block 98, lot 5	Jas Boutwell
Block 99, lot 3	P G Cooper
Block 99, lot 6	Robert McFarland
Block 99, lot 7	Jno L Buell
Block 99, lot 9	A W Harris
Block 100, lot 3	Jno L Buell, Goss Pell & Lowe
Block 100, lot 6	P G Cooper
Block 100, lot 7	Robert McFarland

Block 101, lot 1	Daniel Blocher, A C McBrian
Block 102, lot 7	A W Harris
Block 102, lot 10	Geo H[ackelman], A M W Towner
Block 103, lot 8	Robert McFarland
Block 103, lot 9	P G Cooper
Block 104, lot 3	A W Harris
Block 111, lot 1	Jno L Buell, Goss, Pell & Lowe
Block 111, lot 3	Daniel Williams
Block 111, lot 11	Robert McFarland
Block 111, lot 12	The Aikins [Akins]
Block 112, lot 2	Daniel Williams
Block 112, lot 4	A E Baugh
Block 112, lot 8	P G Cooper
Block 112, lot 12	Chas B Aikens [Akins]
Block 113, lot 3	A E Baugh
Block 113, lot 9	G Hackelman, A M W Towner
Block 114, lot 1	M W Towner
Block 114, lot 2	Chas B Aikens [Akins]
Block 114, lot 12	A E Baugh
Block 115, lot 2	Jno L Buell, Goss Pell & Lowe
Block 115, lot 5	The Aikens [Akins]
Block 115, lot 6	Daniel Williams
Block 115, lot 10	Chas B Aikens [Akins]
Block 115, lot 11	The Aikens [Akins]
Block 116, lot 10	M W Towner
Block 116, lot 12	Jno L Buell, Goss, Pell & Lowe
Block 117, lot 5	M W Towner
Block 118, lot 5	P G Cooper
Block 118, lot 7	Goss, Pell & Co
Block 118, lot 8	Daniel Williams
Block 118, lot 11	A E Baugh
Block 119, lot 1	M W Towner
Block 119, lot 4	Goss, Pell & Lowe
Block 119, lot 10	Chas B Aikens [Akins]

Block 119, lot 11	Thomas Aikins [Akins]
Block 119, lot 12	A W Harris
Block 120, lot 3	A E Baugh
Block 121, lot 4	Chas B Aikens [Akins]
Block 121, lot 5	The Aikins [Akins]
Block 121, lot 6	Daniel Williams
Block 121, lot 8	William Mills
Block 121, lot 9	Geo Hackelman, M W Towner
Block 121, lot 12	A B Parrington, Franklin Mays
Block 122, lot 5	A M Hunt
Block 123, lot 3	Chas B Aikens [Akins]
Block 124, lot 5	M W Towner
Block 124, lot 7	Geo Hackelman, A M W Towner
Block 124, lot 10	Jno L Buell, Goss, Pell & Lowe
Block 145, lot 4	A E Baugh
Block 145, lot 11	Jno L Buell, Goss, Pell & Lowe
Block 145, lot 12	M W Towner
Block 146, lot 5	Chas B Aikens [Akins]
Block 146, lot 10	Daniel Williams
Block 147, lot 1	Jno L Buell, Goss, Pell & Lowe
Block 147, lot 2	Jno L Buell, Goss, Pell & Lowe
Block 147, lot 12	Geo Hackelman, A M W Towner
Block 149, lot 1	Chas B Aikens [Akins]
Block 149, lot 2	M W Towner
Block 149, lot 12	Robert McFarland
Block 151, lot 4	Geo Hackelman, A M W Towner
Block 151, lot 6	A E Baugh
Block 151, lot 8	Chas B Aikens [Akins]
Block 152, lot 5	A M Hunt
Block 152, lot 8	Jno Buell, Goss, Pell & Lowe
Block 152, lot 12	A W Harris
Block 153, lot 1	Daniel Williams
Block 153, lot 12	A W Harris (crossed out)
Block 154, lot 11	M W Towner

Block 156, lot 6	A M Hunt
Block 157, lot 3	A W Harris
Block 157, lot 9	Geo Hackelman, A M W Towner
Block 158, lot 5	Robert McFarland
Block 158, lot 8	P G Cooper
Block 165, lot 1	P G Cooper
Block 165, lot 4	A M Hunt
Block 166, lot 6	Robert McFarland
Block 166, lot 12	Geo Hackelman, A M W Towner
Block 167, lot 10	A W Harris
Block 168, lot 5	A W Harris
Block 169, lot 6	A W Harris
Block 169, lot 10	P G Cooper
Block 169, lot 11	Robert McFarland
Block 170, lot 3	Robert McFarland
Block 170, lot 4	P G Cooper
Block 170, lot 7	A M Hunt
Block 171, lot 5	Geo Hackelman, A M W Towner
Block 172, lot 10	Chas B Aikens [Akins]
Block 173, lot 11	A E Baugh
Block 174, lot 4	M W Towner
Block 174, lot 10	Daniel Williams
Block 175, lot 3	Chas B Aikens [Akins]
Block 175, lot 10	M W Towner
Block 176, lot 2	A E Baugh
Block 176, lot 11	Jno L Buell, Goss, Pell & Lowe
Block 178, lot 3	Daniel Williams
Block 178, lot 7	A W Harris
Block 178, lot 11	Daniel Williams

1–6

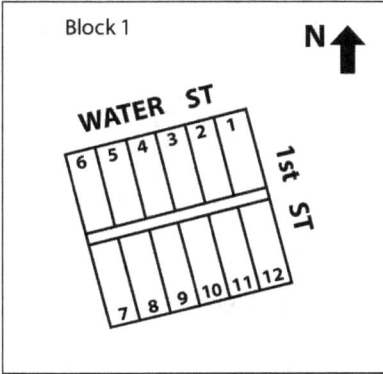

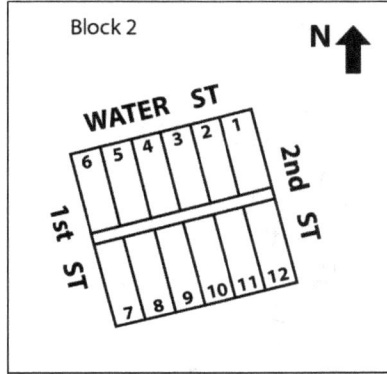

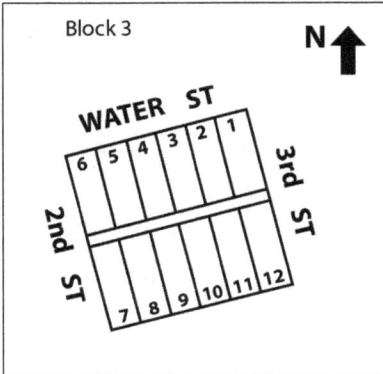

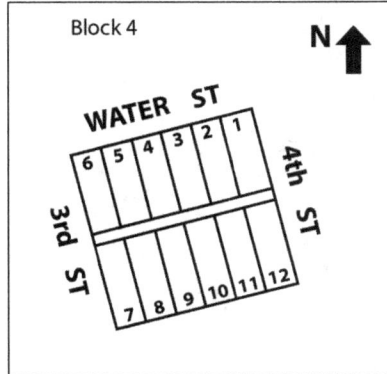

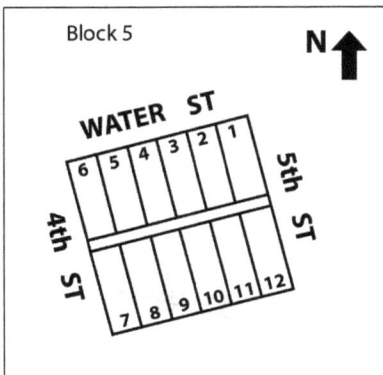

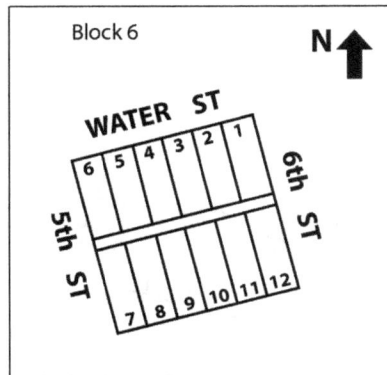

7–12

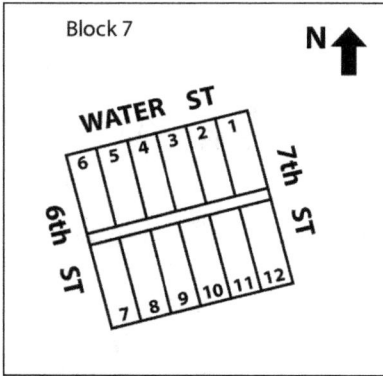

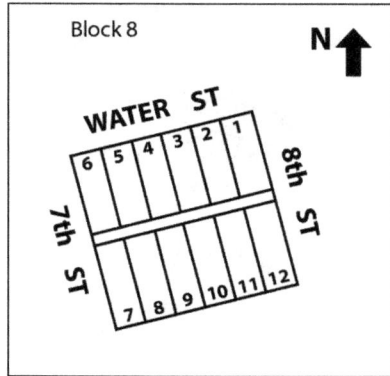

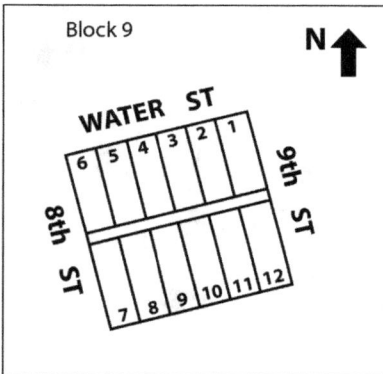

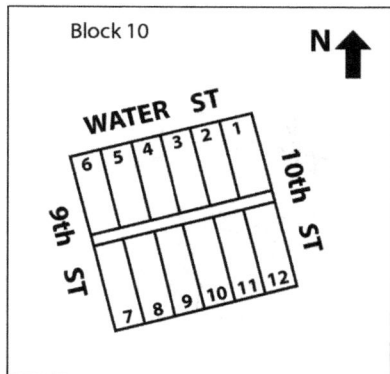

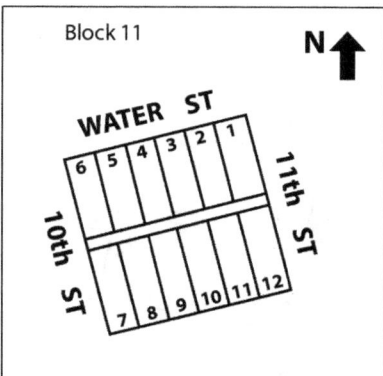

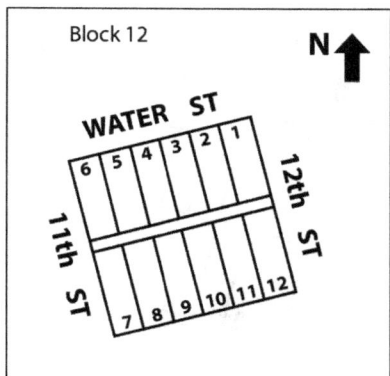

13–18

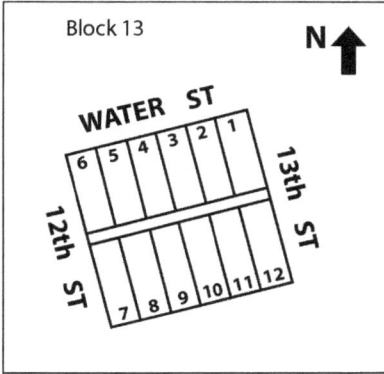

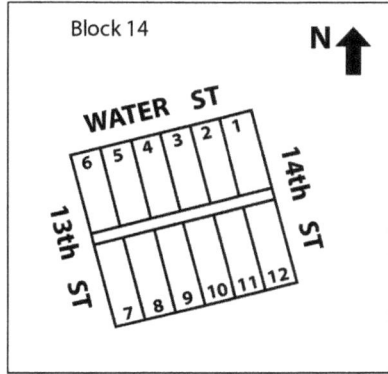

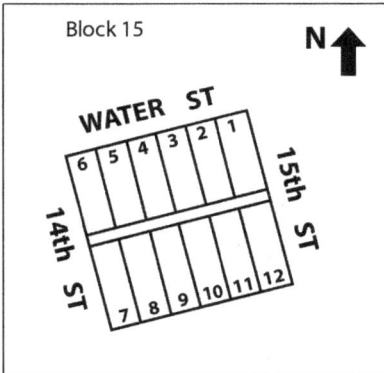

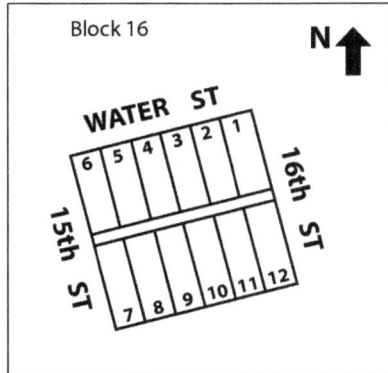

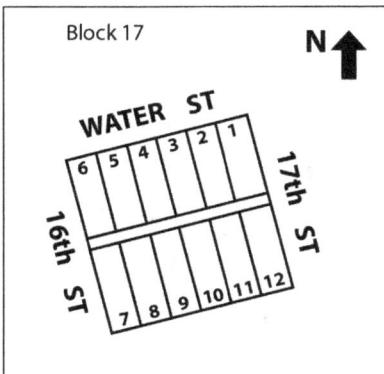

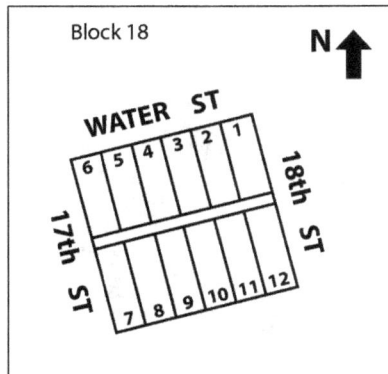

19–24

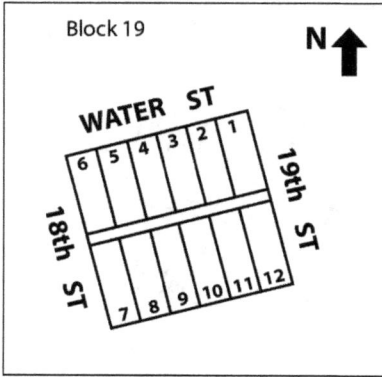

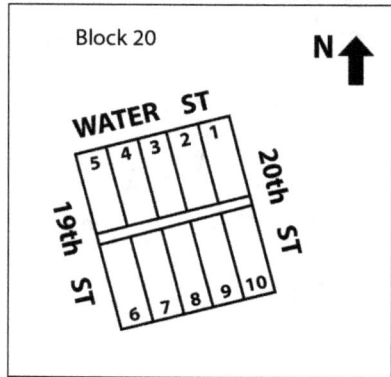

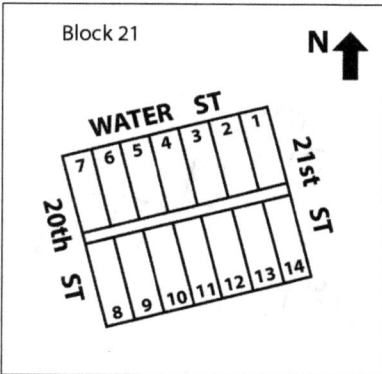

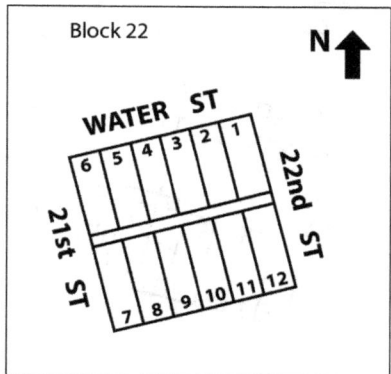

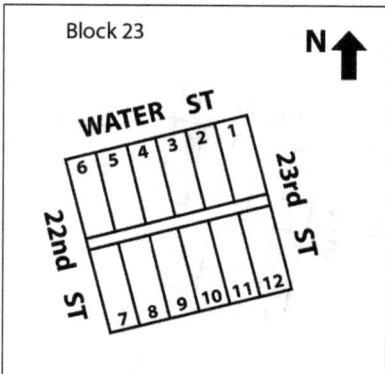

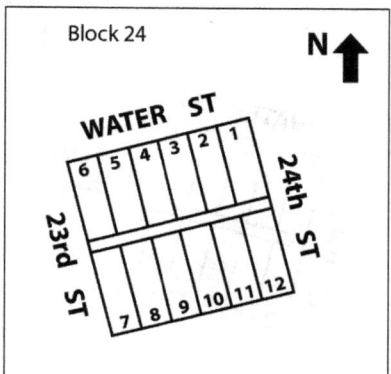

25–30

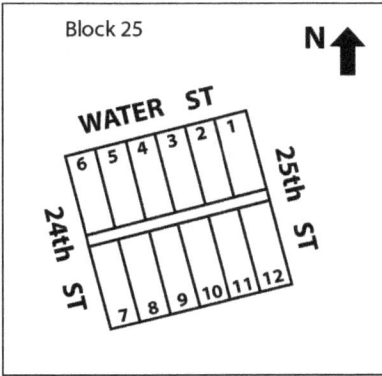

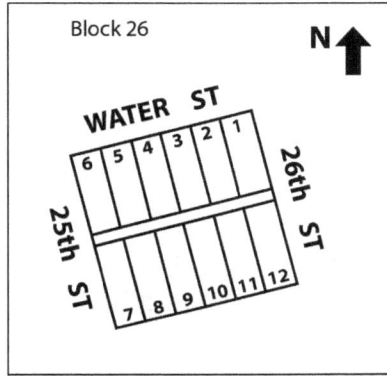

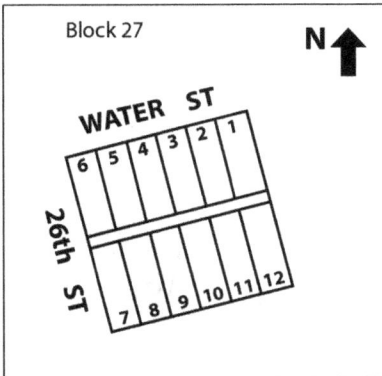

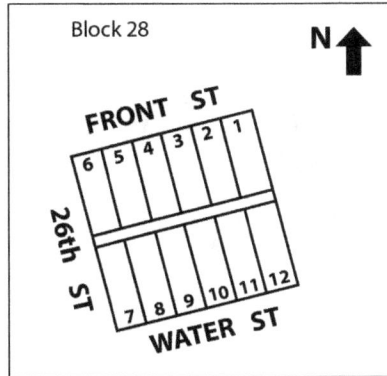

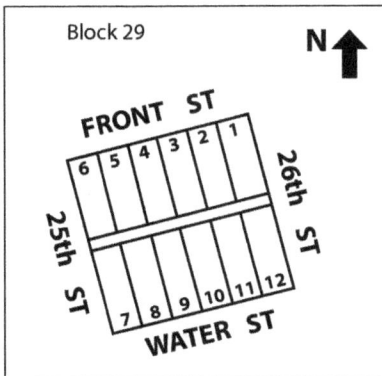

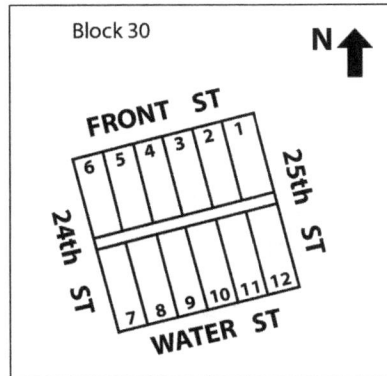

31–36

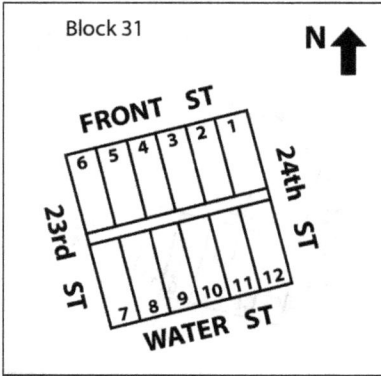

Block 31

N

FRONT ST
6 5 4 3 2 1
23rd ST
24th ST
7 8 9 10 11 12
WATER ST

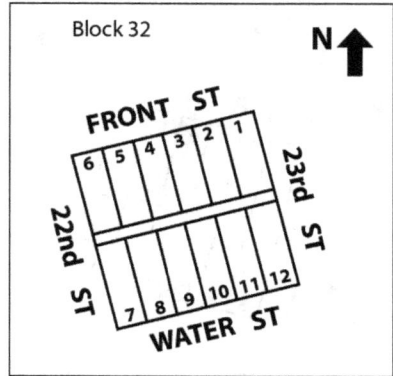

Block 32

N

FRONT ST
6 5 4 3 2 1
22nd ST
23rd ST
7 8 9 10 11 12
WATER ST

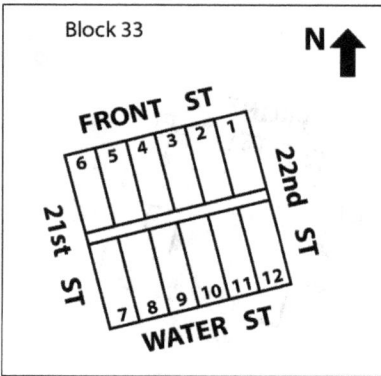

Block 33

N

FRONT ST
6 5 4 3 2 1
21st ST
22nd ST
7 8 9 10 11 12
WATER ST

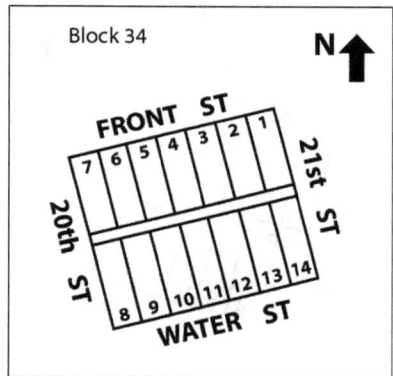

Block 34

N

FRONT ST
7 6 5 4 3 2 1
20th ST
21st ST
8 9 10 11 12 13 14
WATER ST

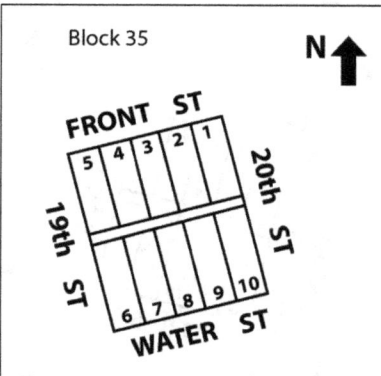

Block 35

N

FRONT ST
5 4 3 2 1
19th ST
20th ST
6 7 8 9 10
WATER ST

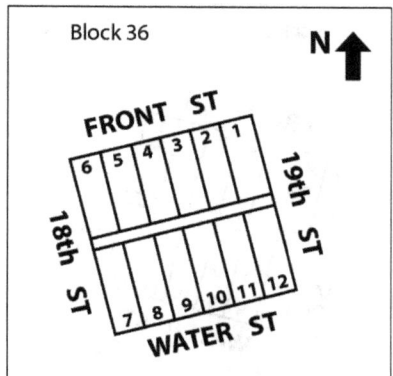

Block 36

N

FRONT ST
6 5 4 3 2 1
18th ST
19th ST
7 8 9 10 11 12
WATER ST

37–42

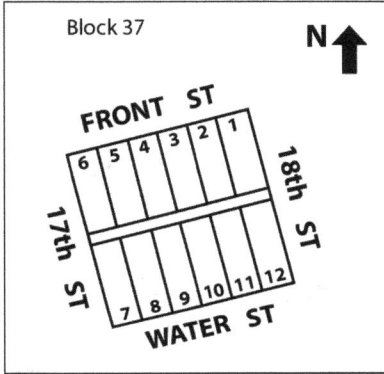

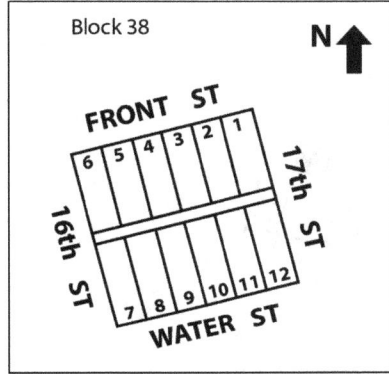

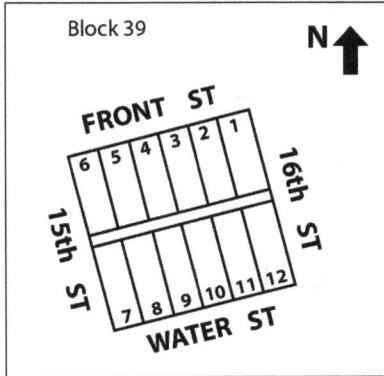

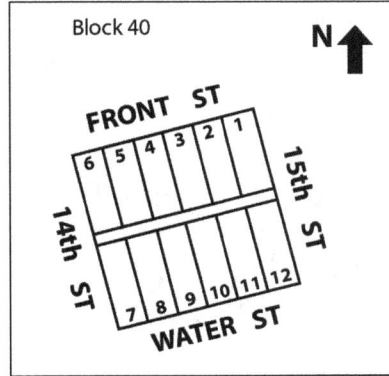

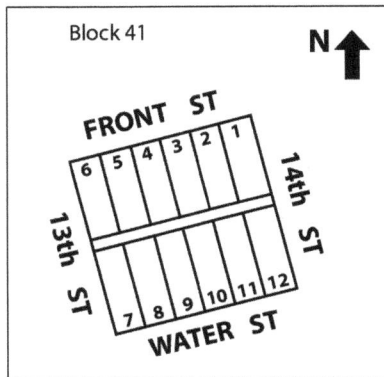

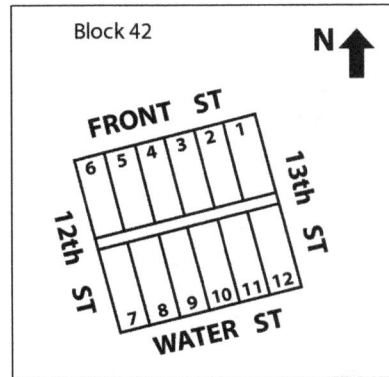

43–48

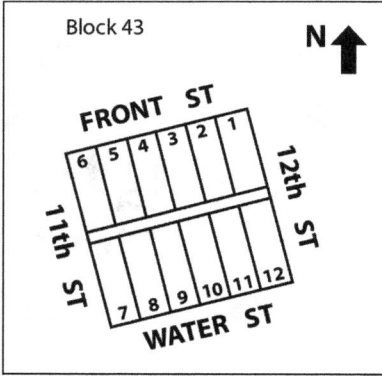

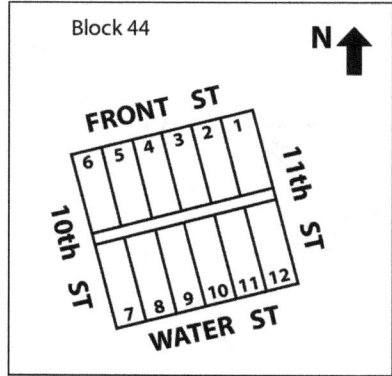

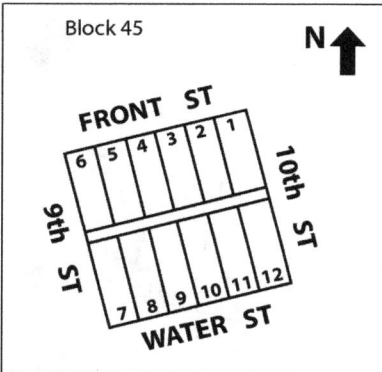

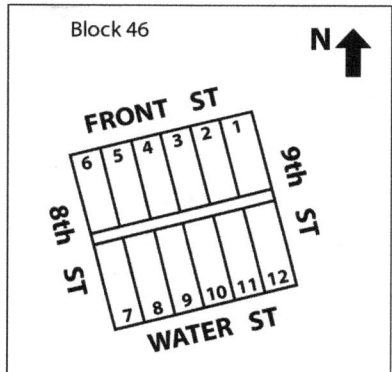

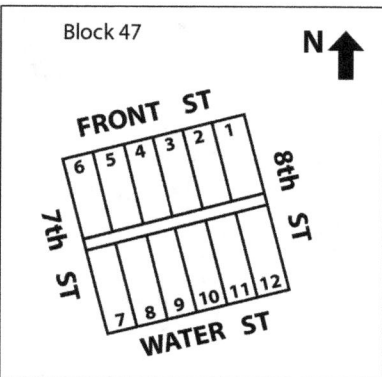

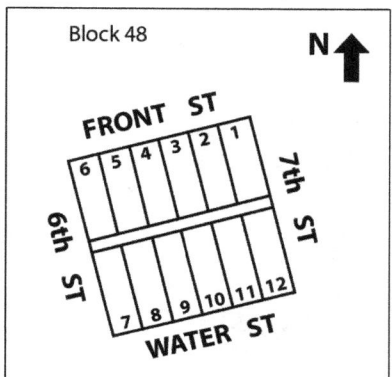

49–54

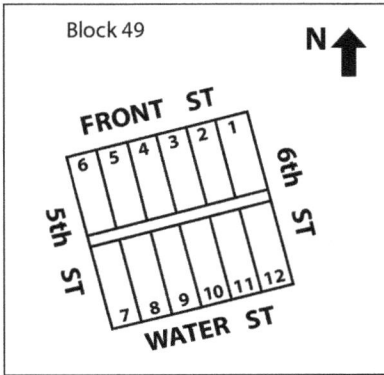

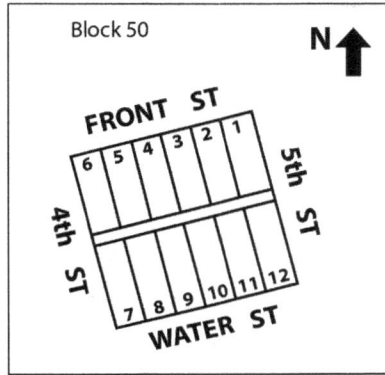

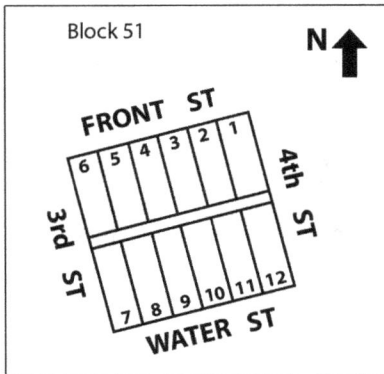

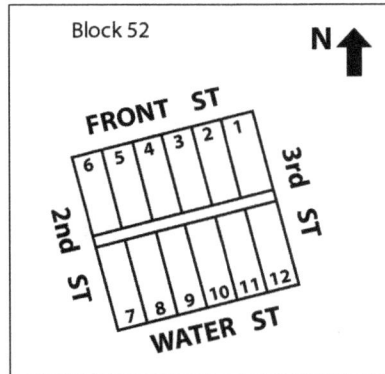

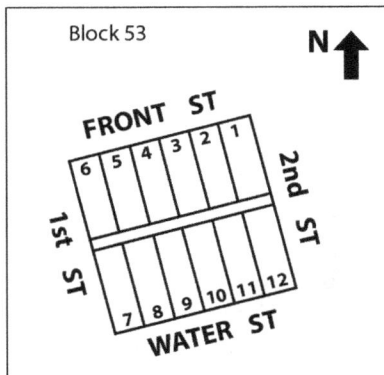

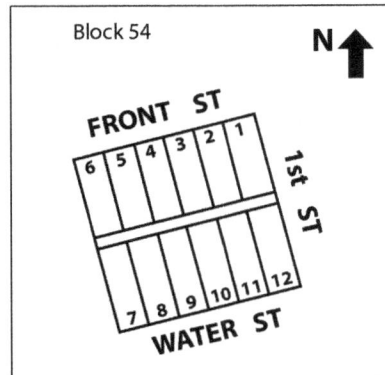

55–60

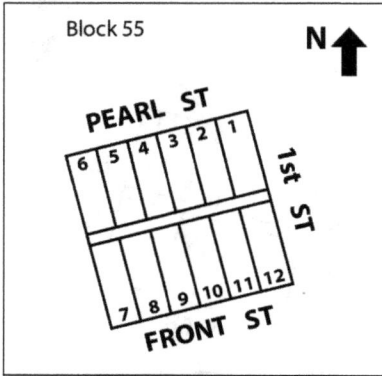

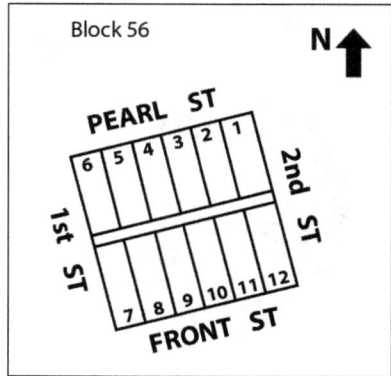

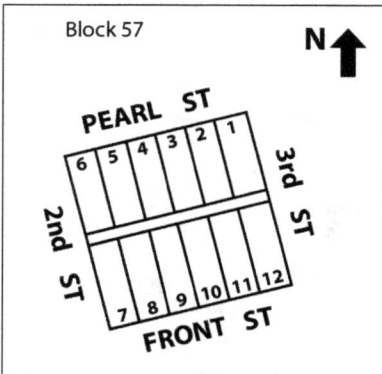

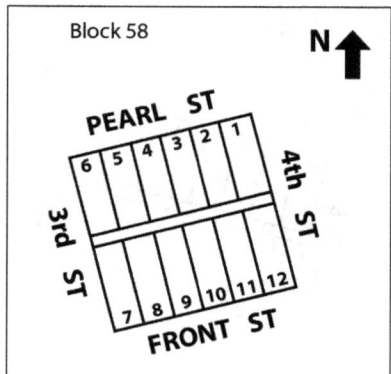

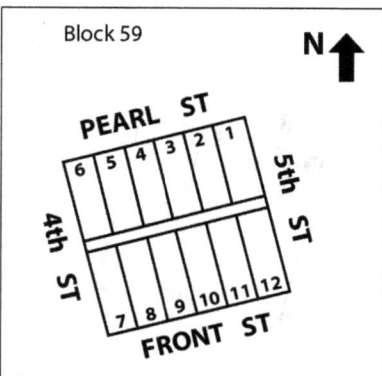

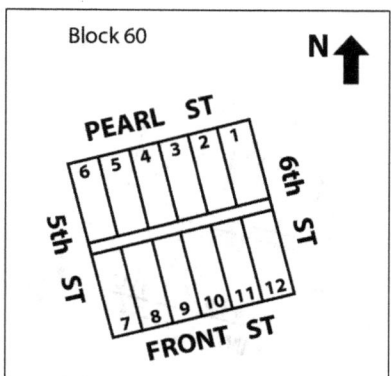

61–66

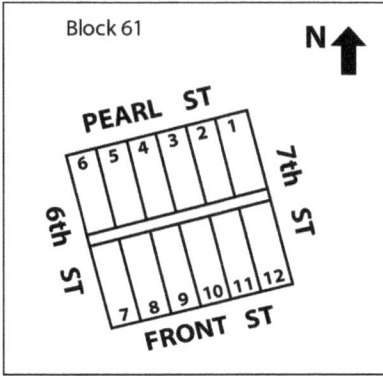

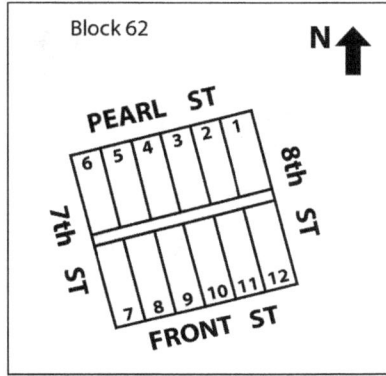

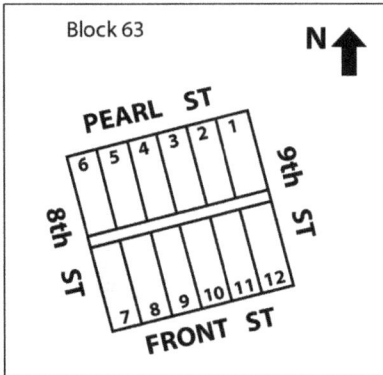

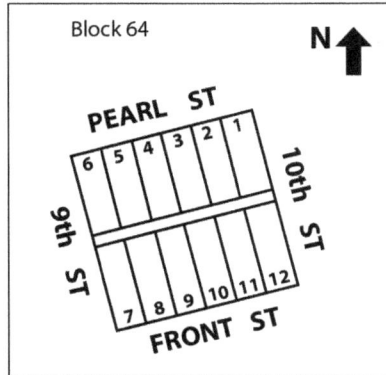

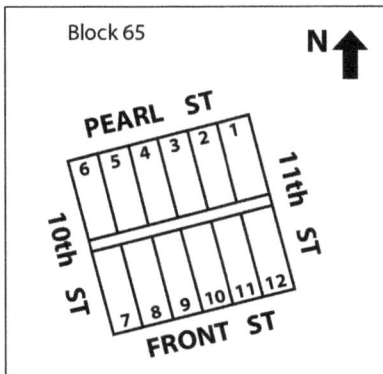

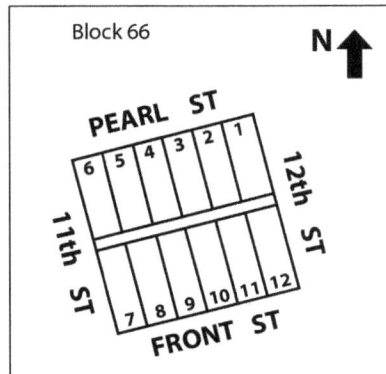

67–72

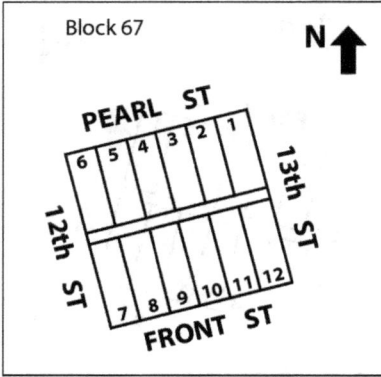

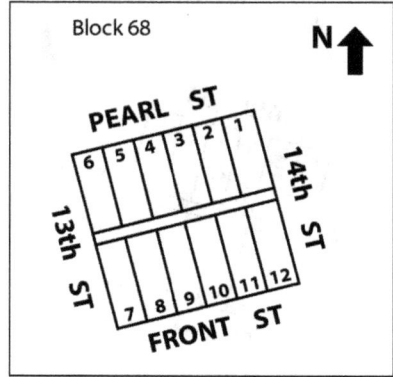

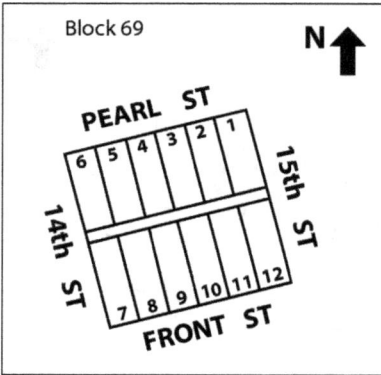

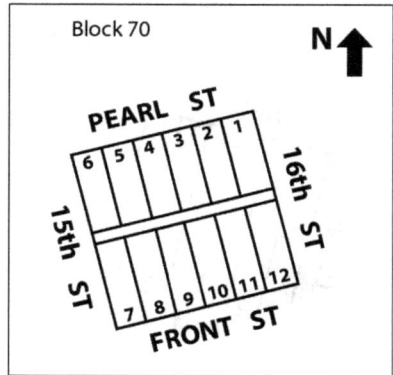

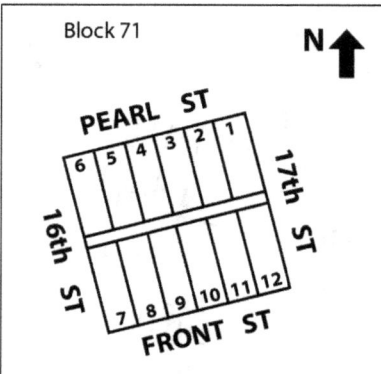

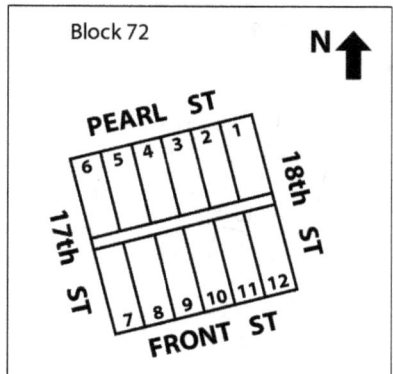

73–78

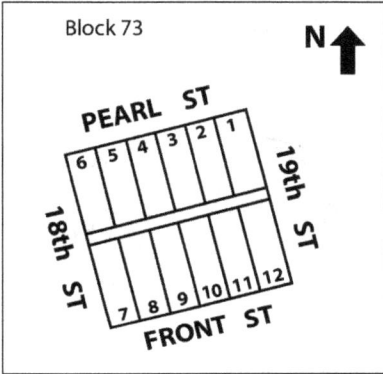

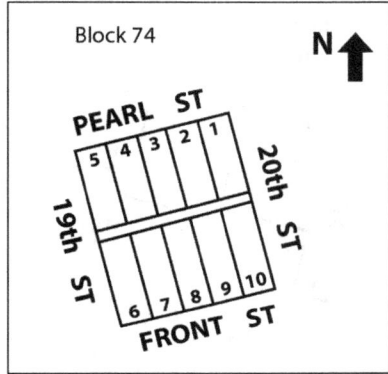

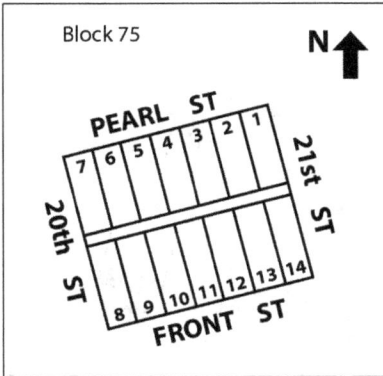

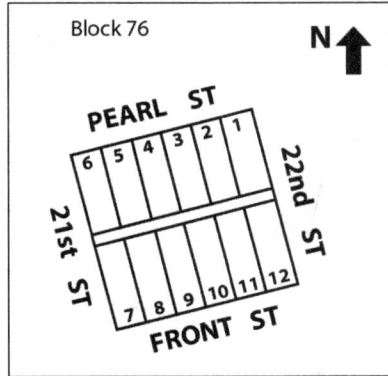

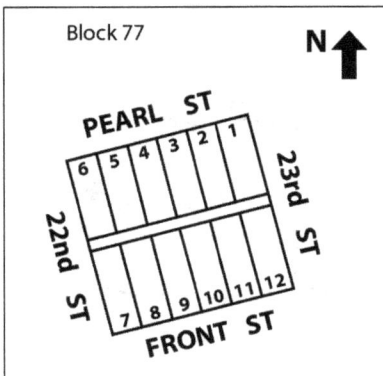

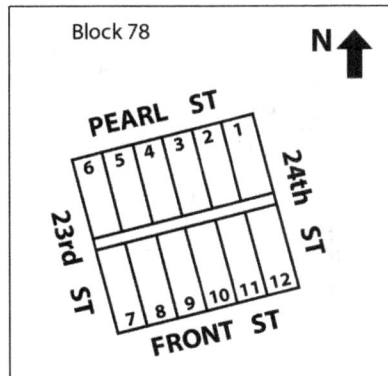

79–84

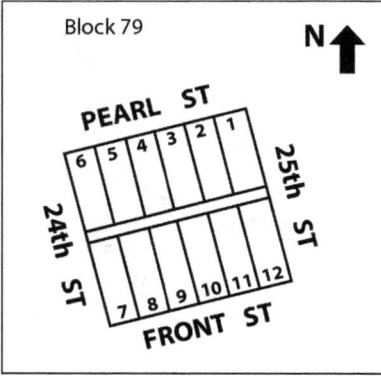

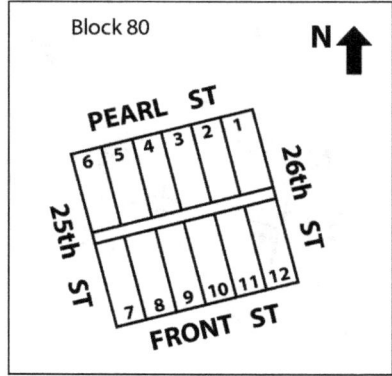

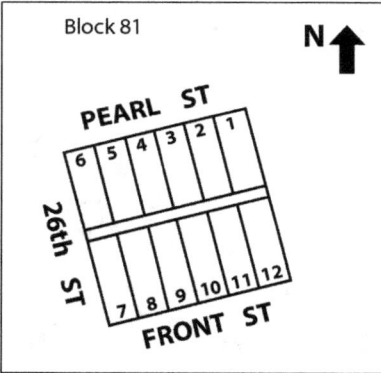

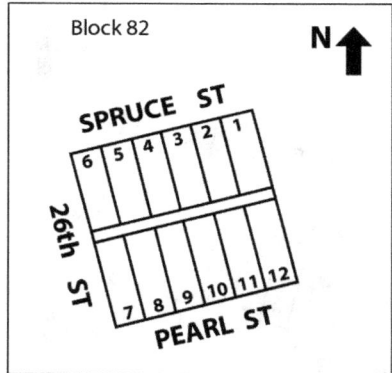

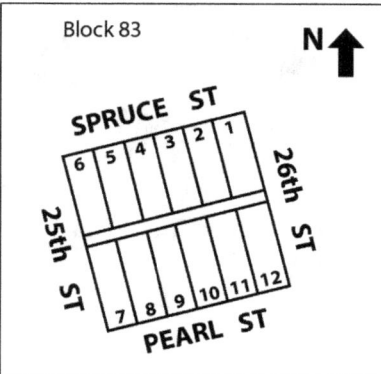

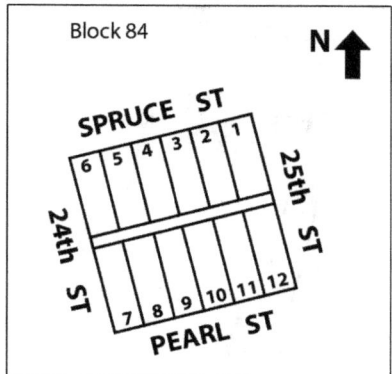

85–90

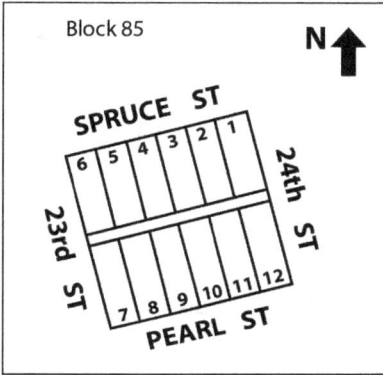

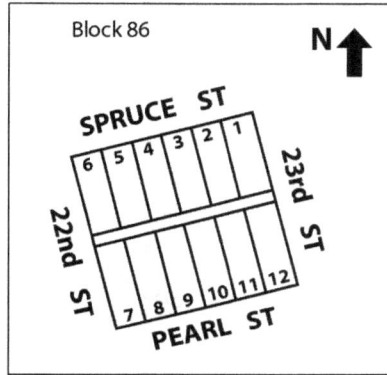

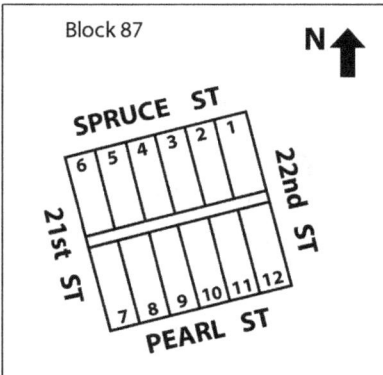

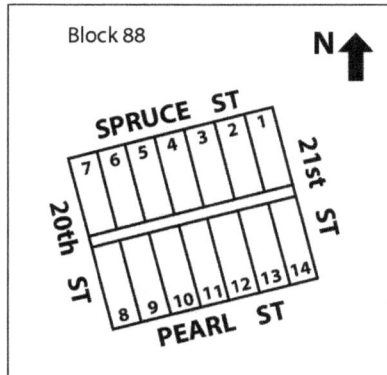

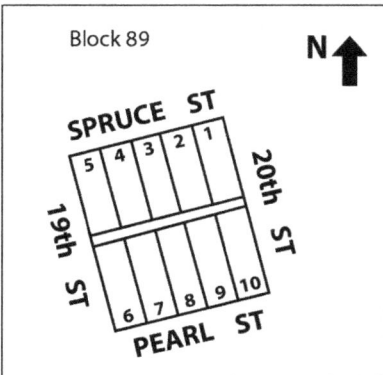

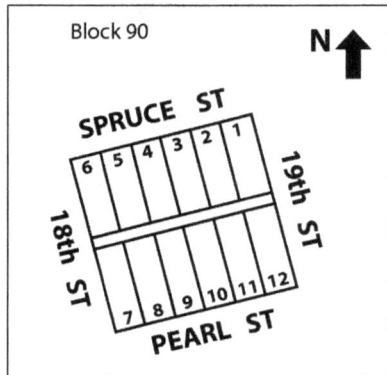

91–96

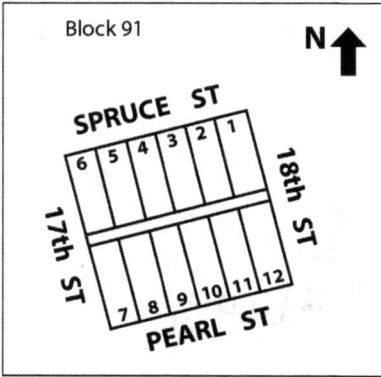

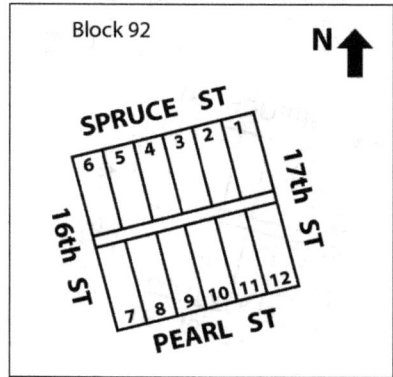

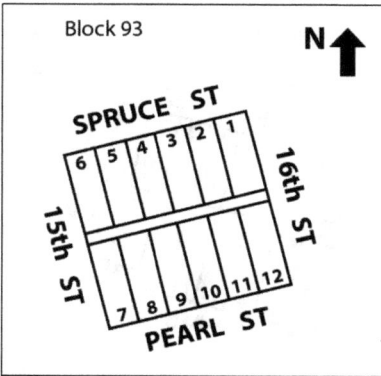

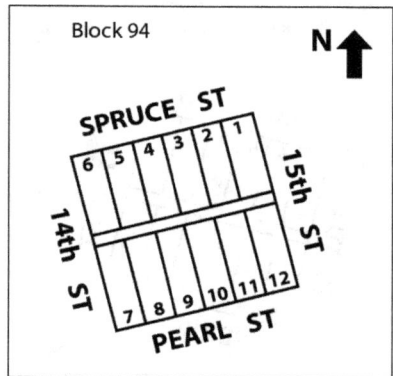

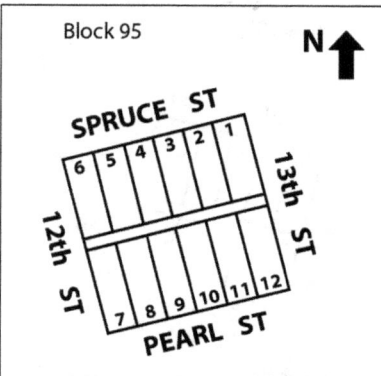

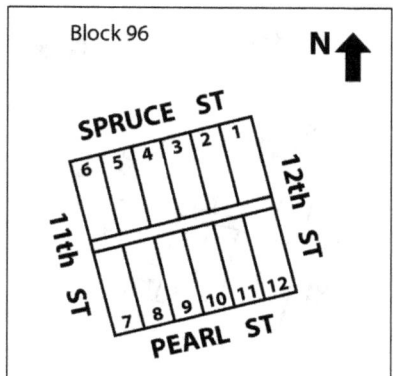

97–102

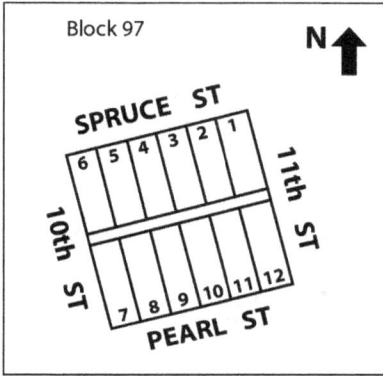

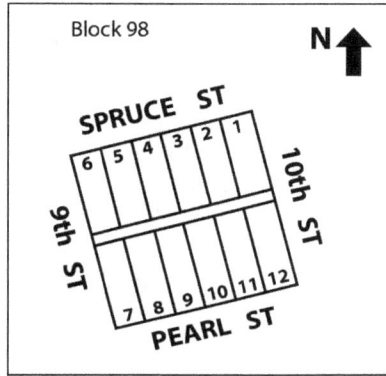

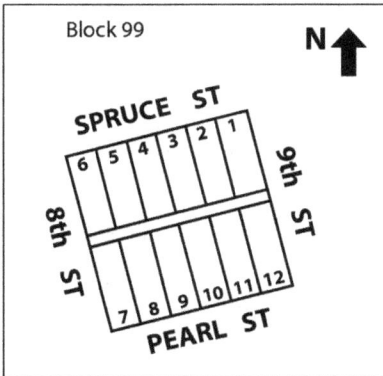

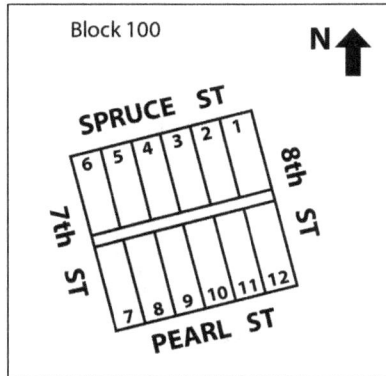

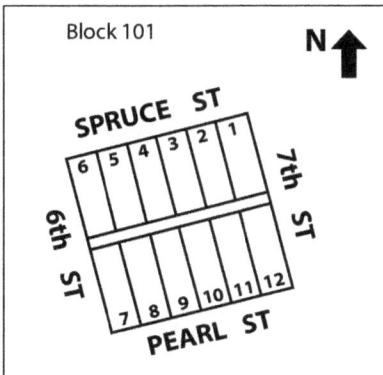

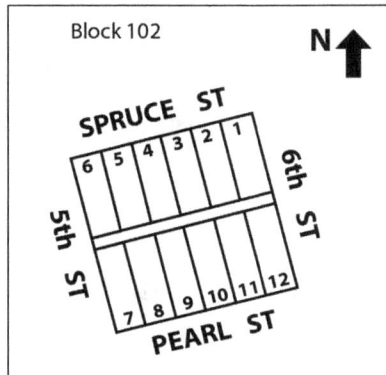

103–108

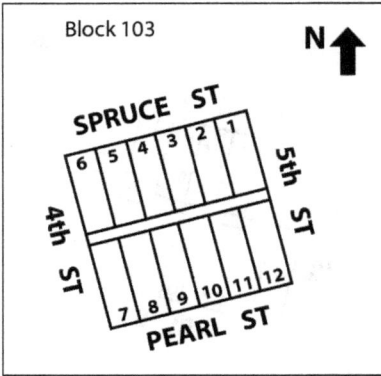

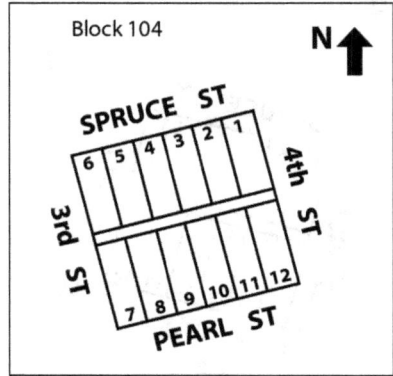

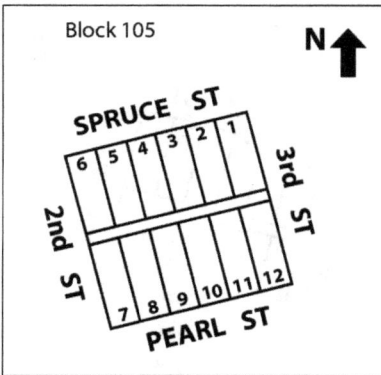

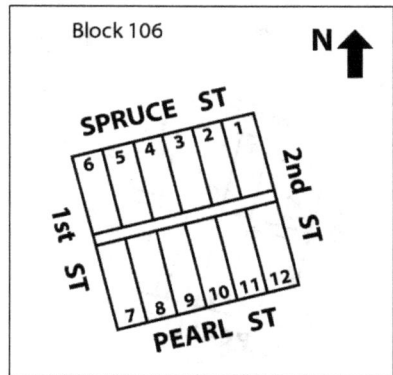

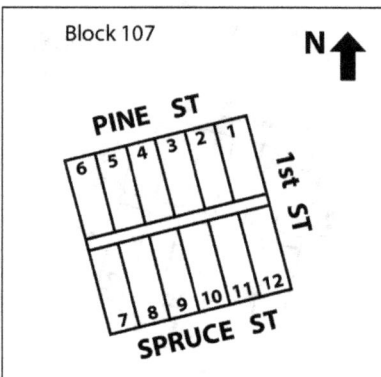

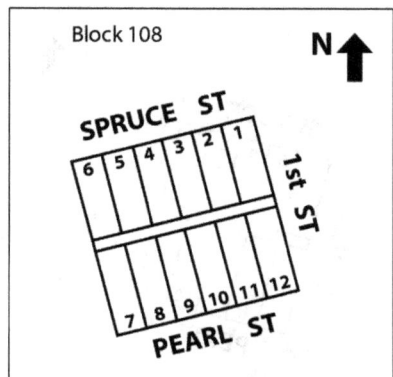

109–114

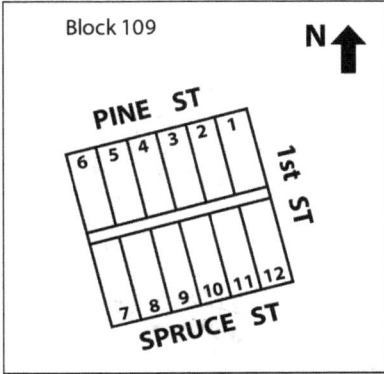

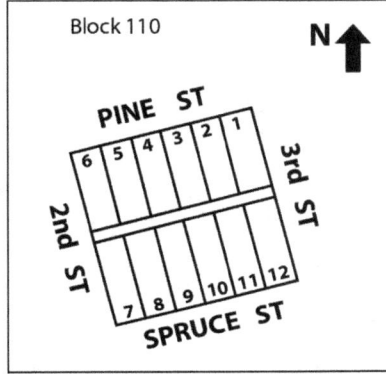

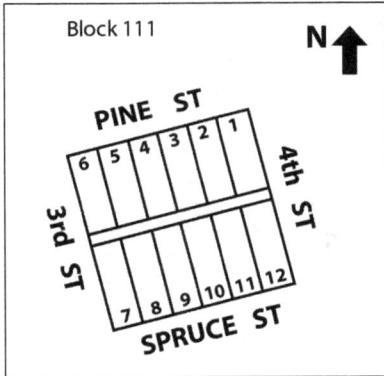

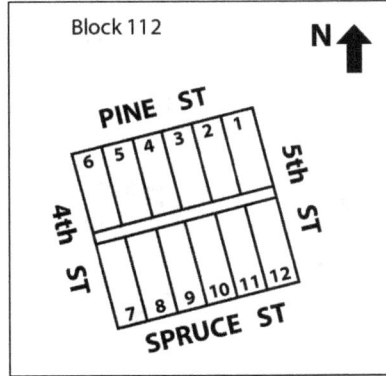

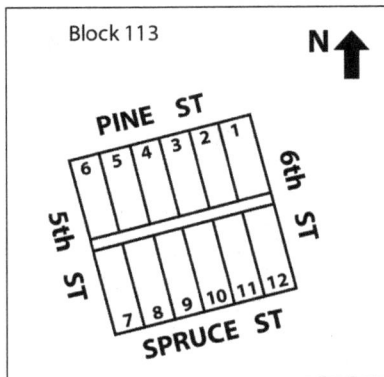

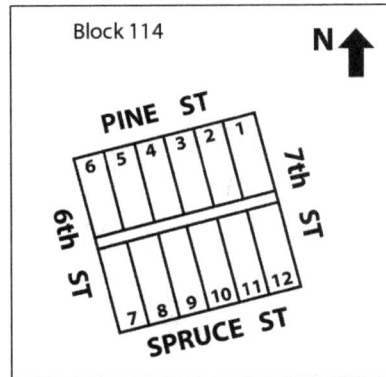

115–120

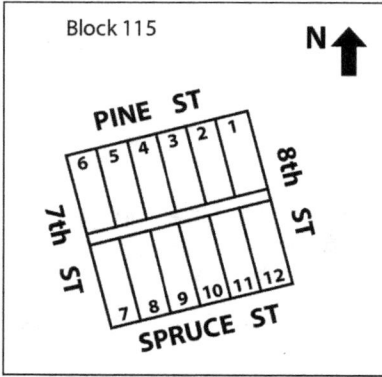

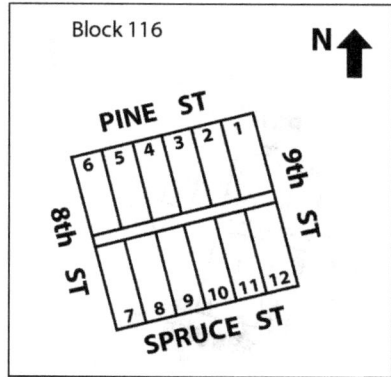

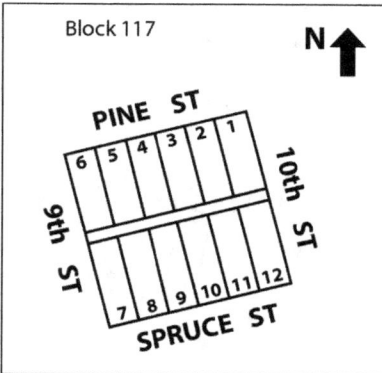

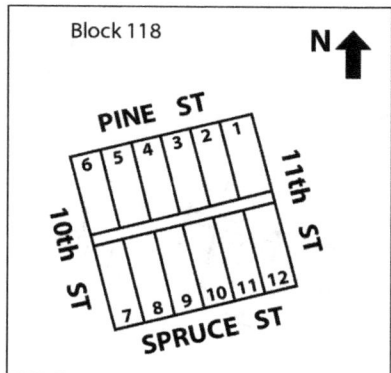

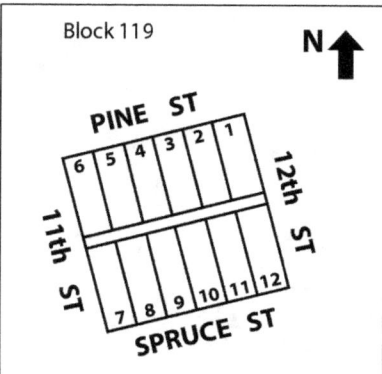

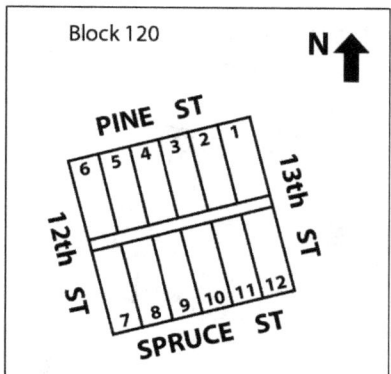

121–126

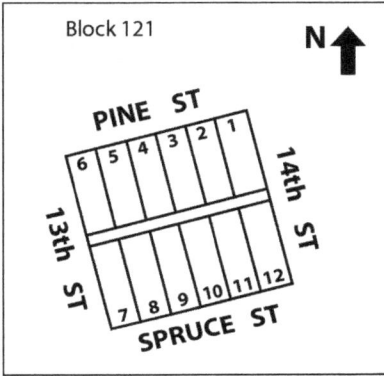

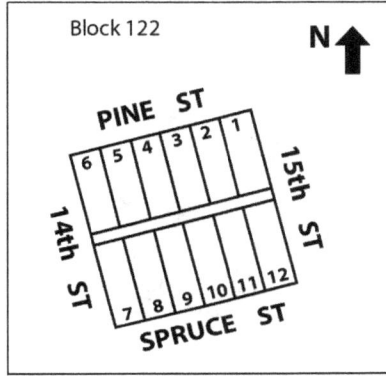

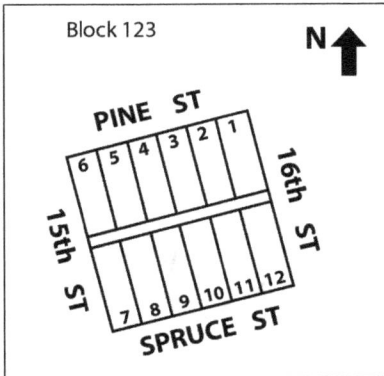

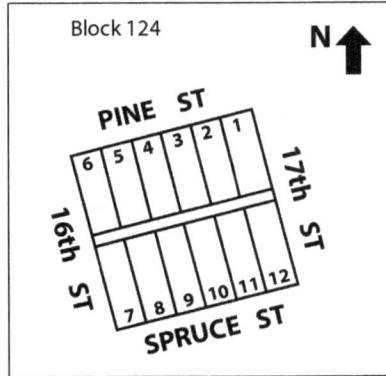

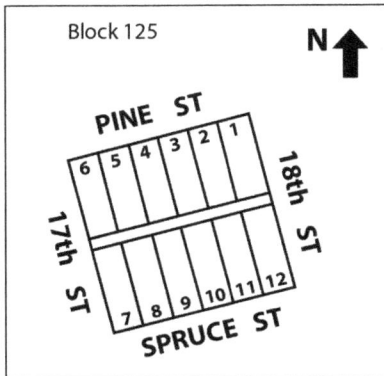

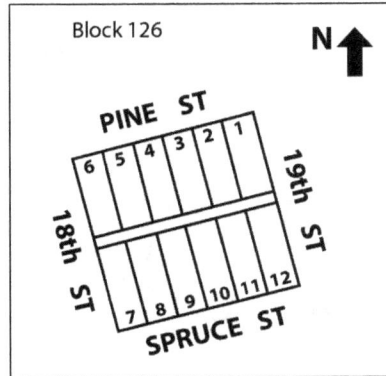

127–132

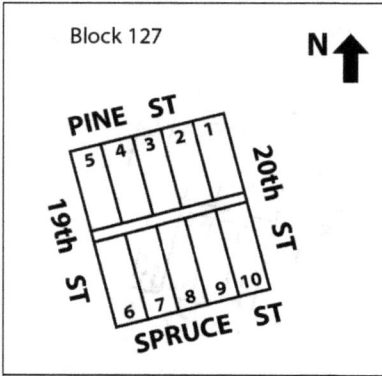

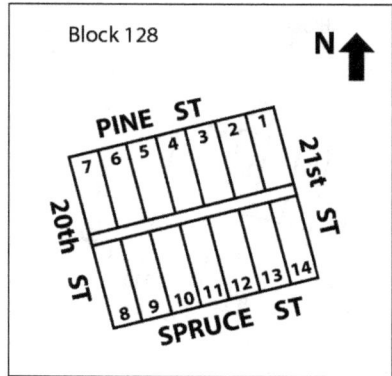

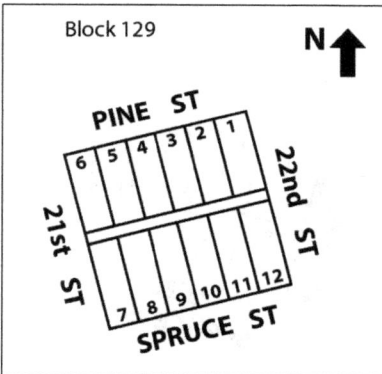

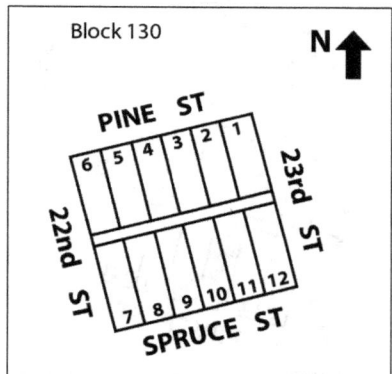

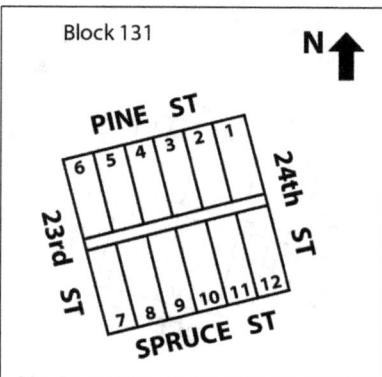

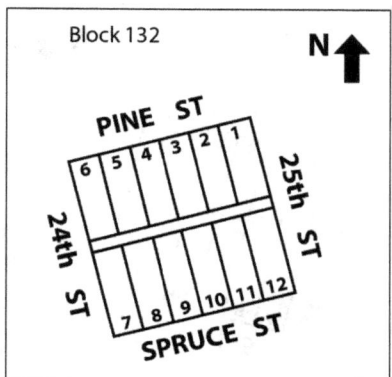

133–138

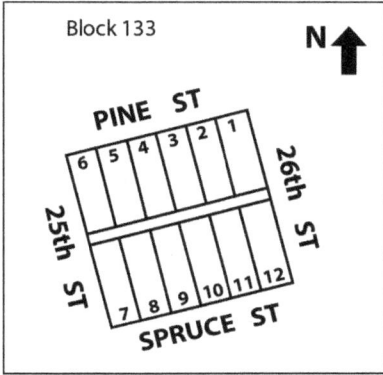

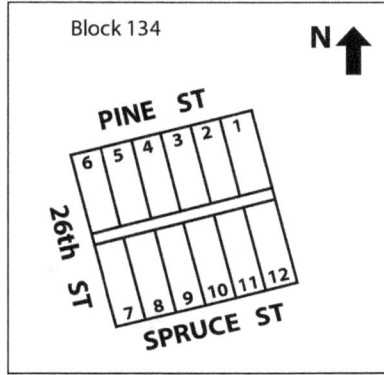

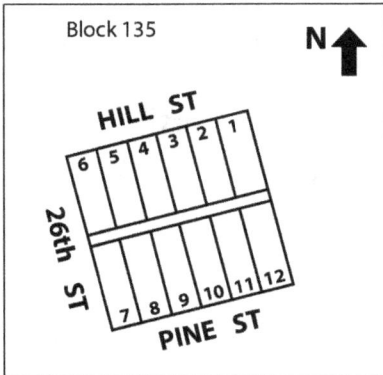

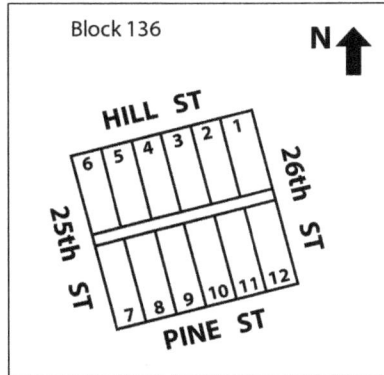

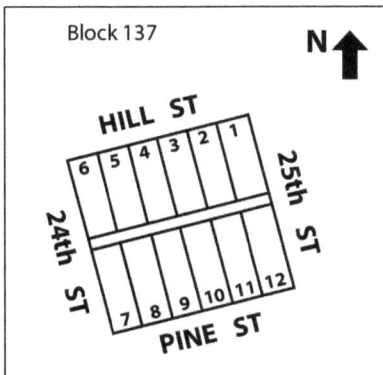

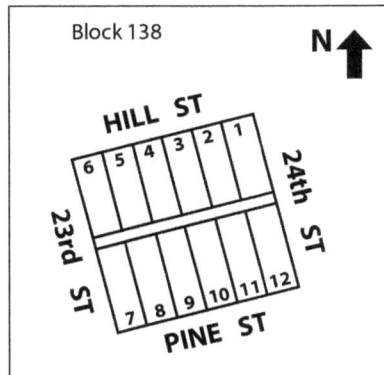

139–144

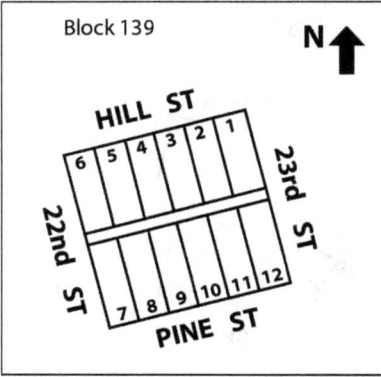

Block 139

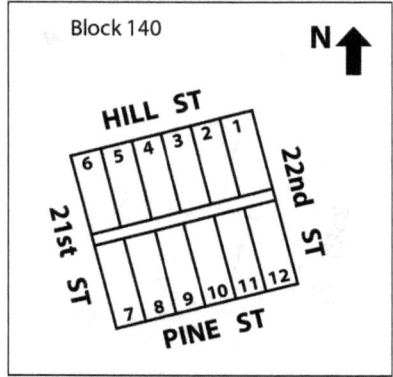

Block 140

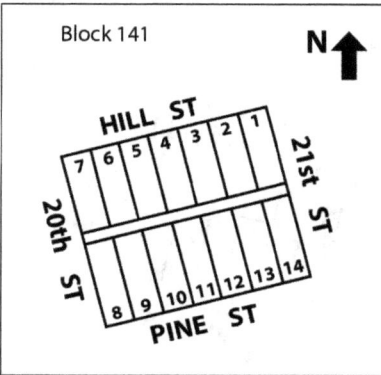

Block 141

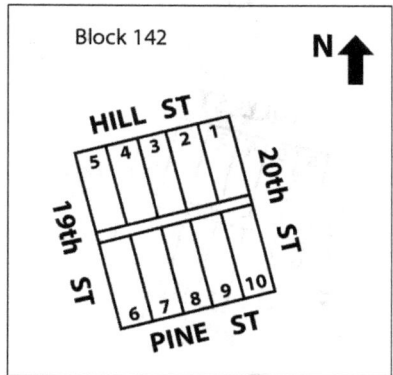

Block 142

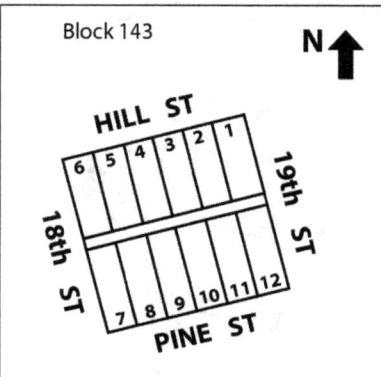

Block 143

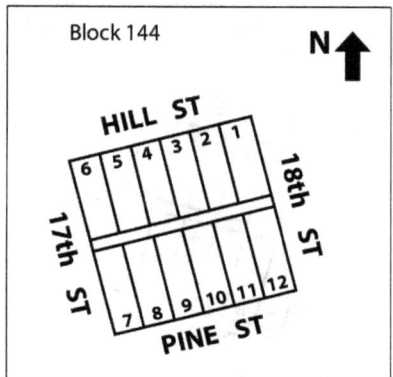

Block 144

145–150

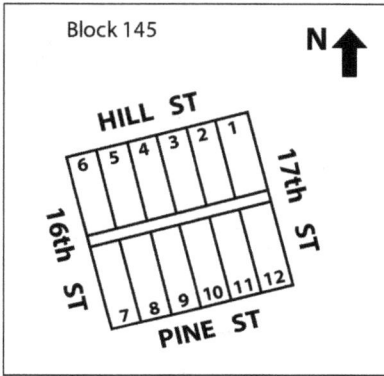

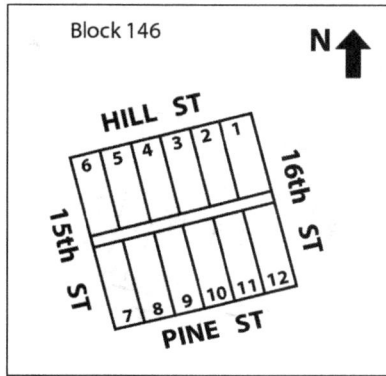

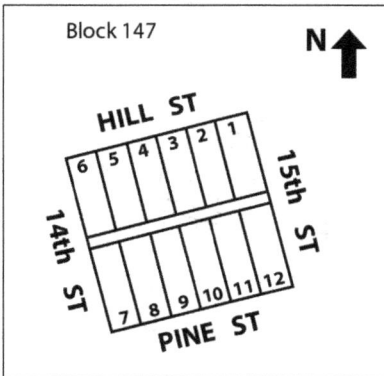

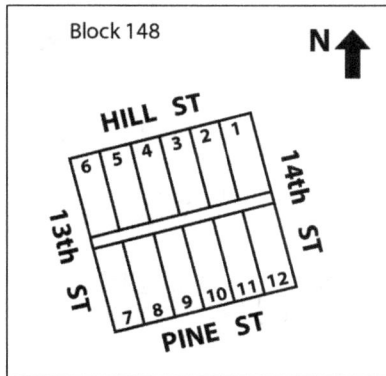

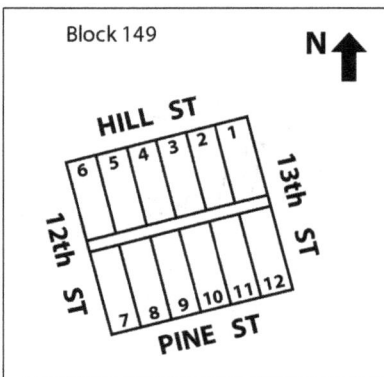

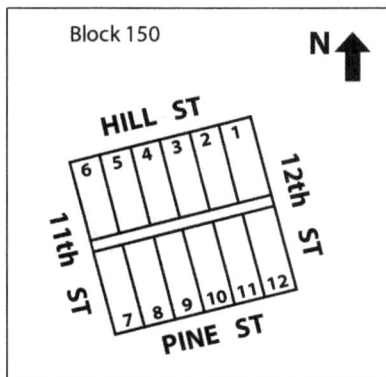

151–156

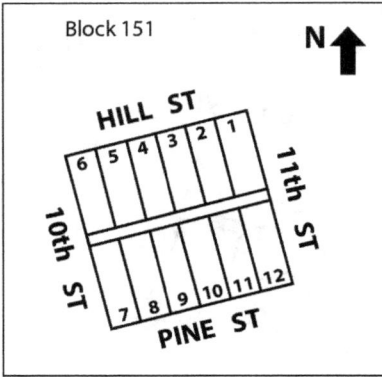

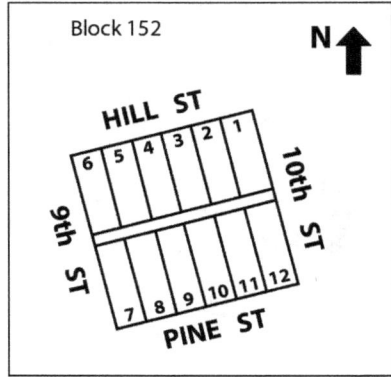

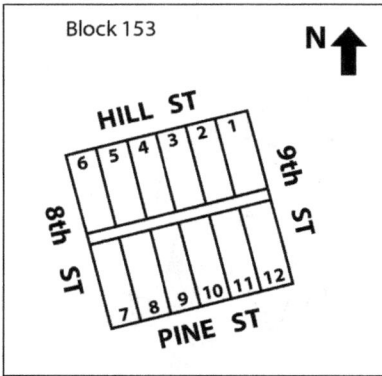

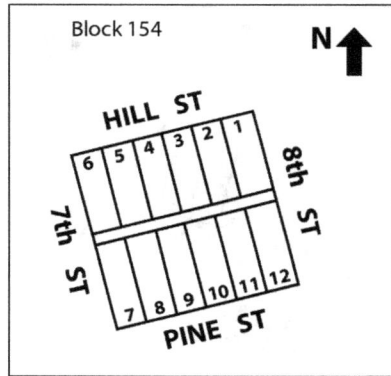

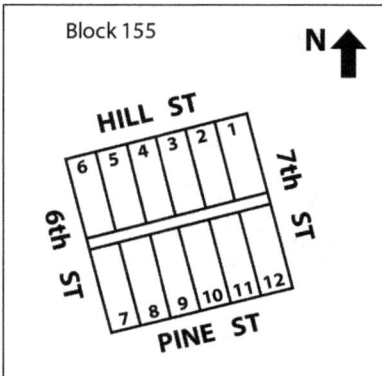

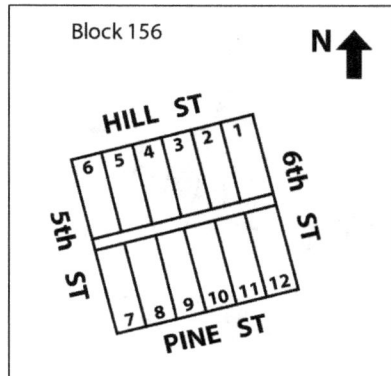

157–162

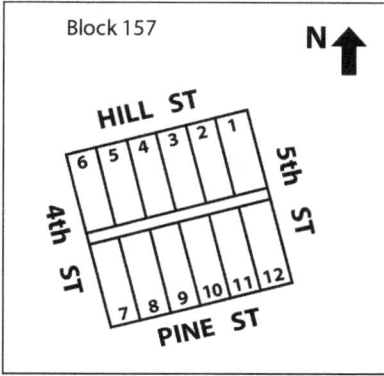

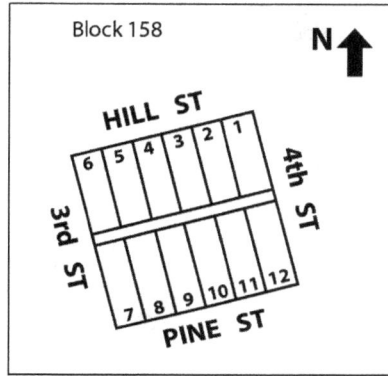

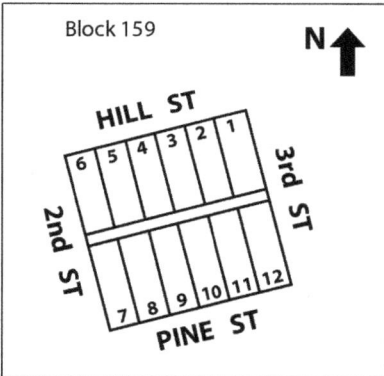

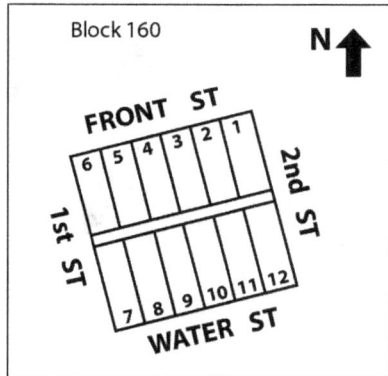

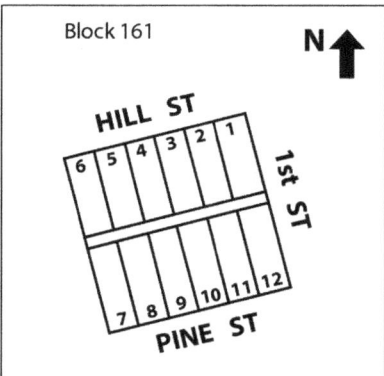

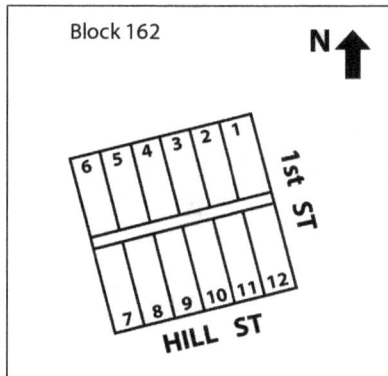

163–168

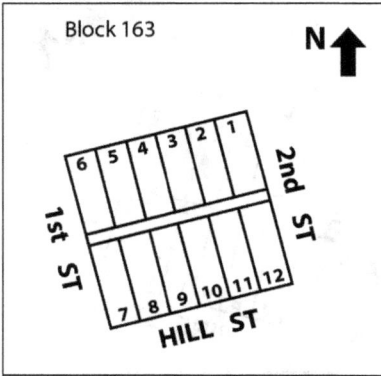

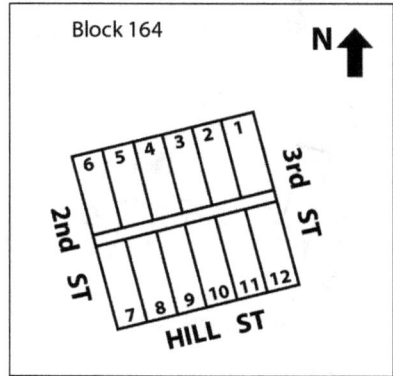

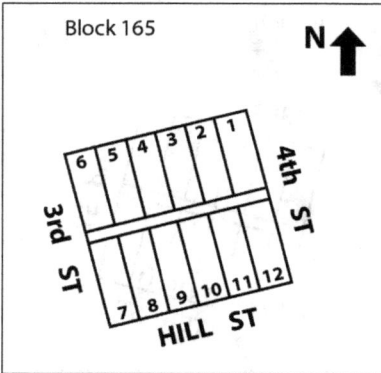

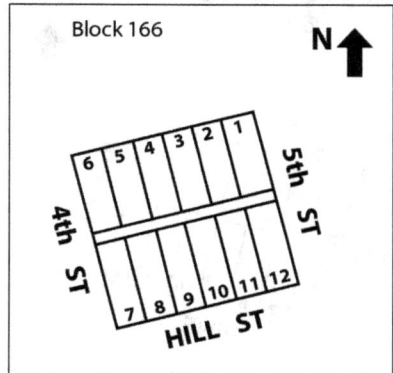

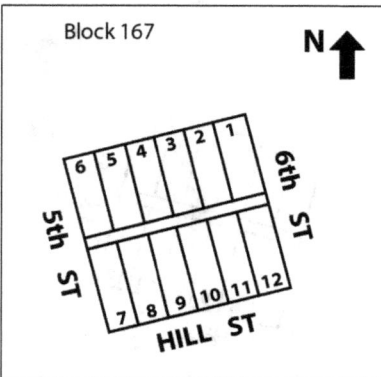

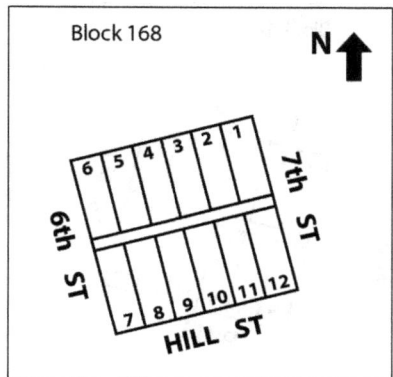

169–174

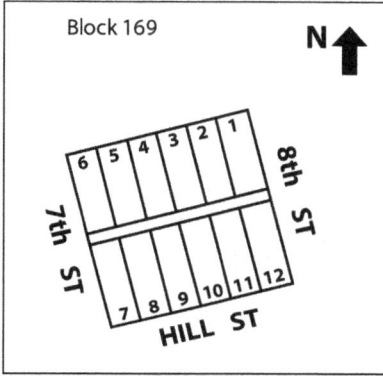

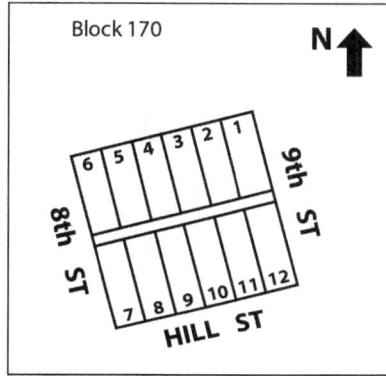

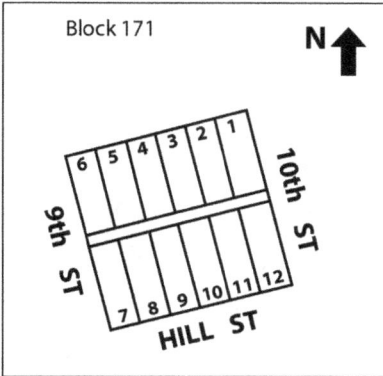

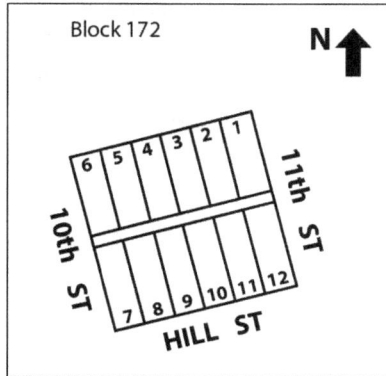

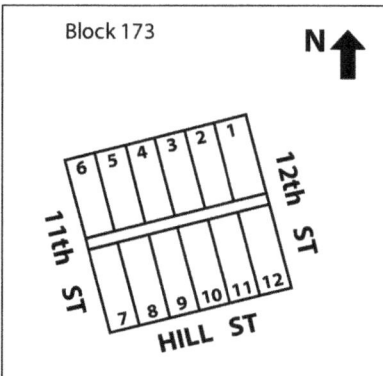

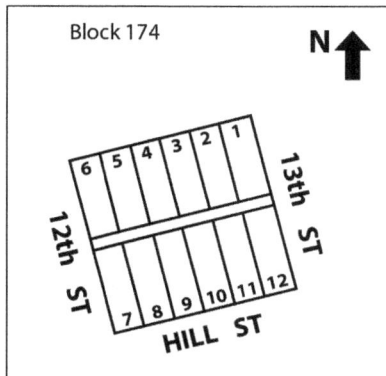

175–180

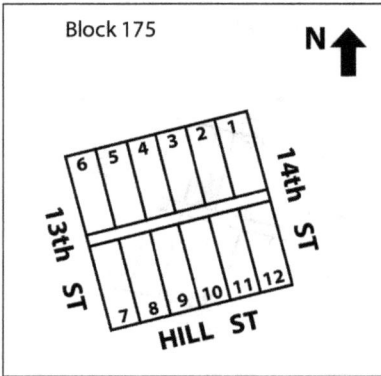

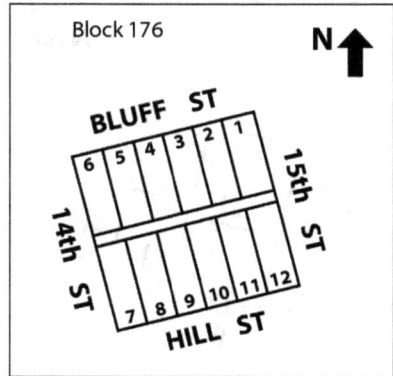

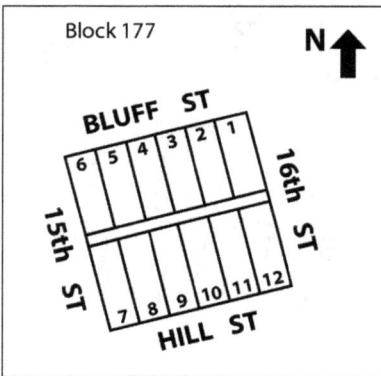

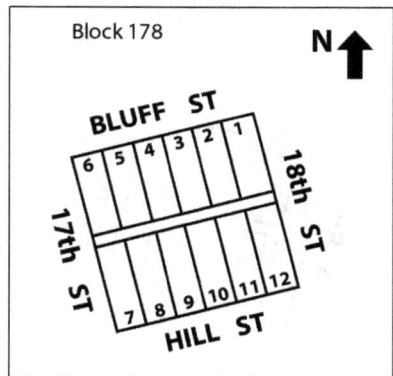

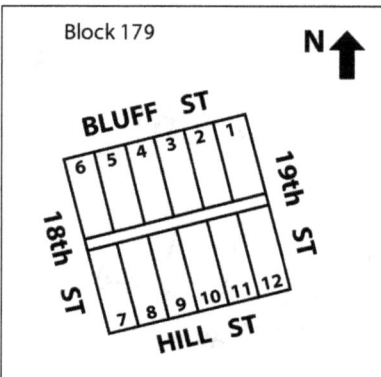

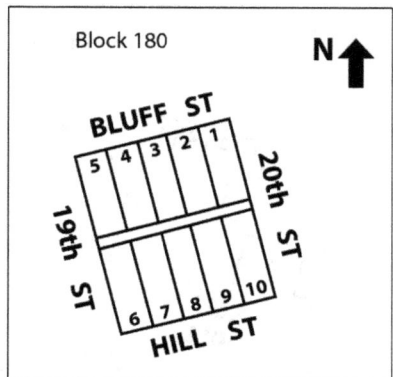

181–186

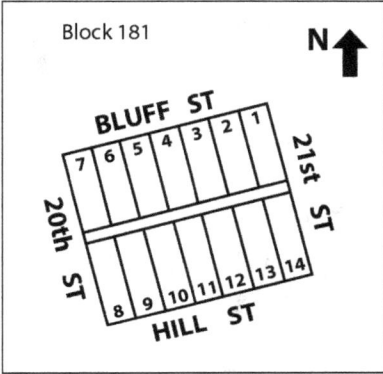

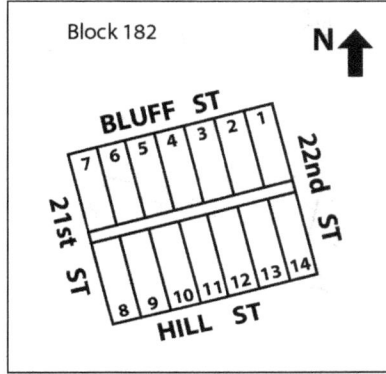

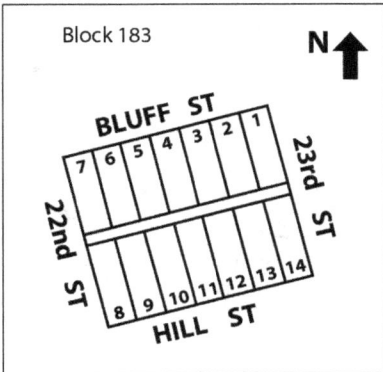

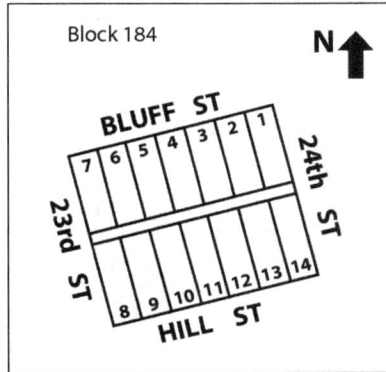

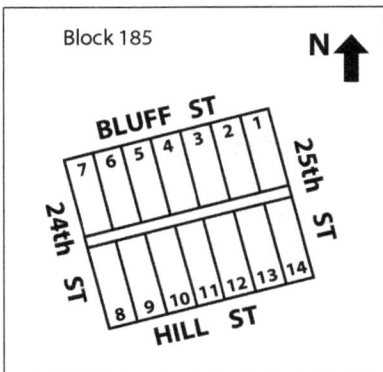

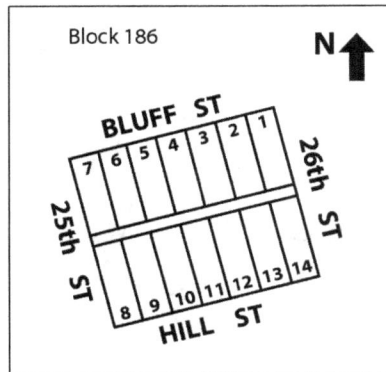

187–192

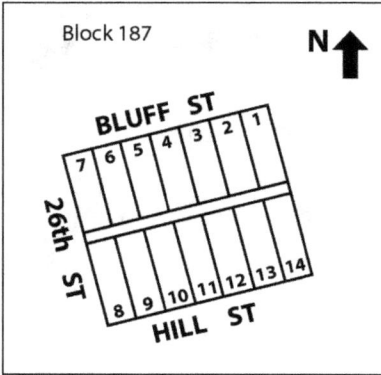

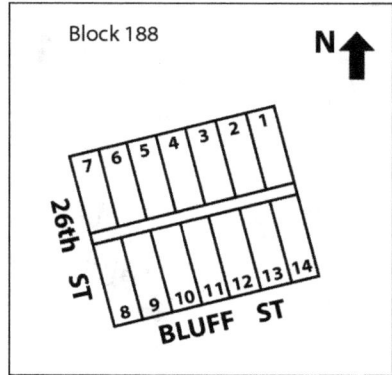

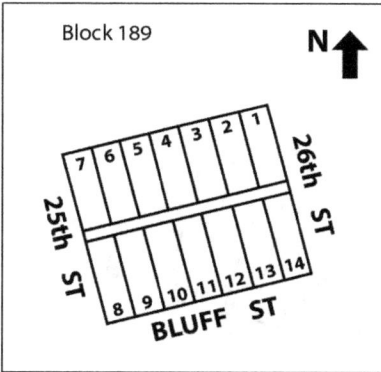

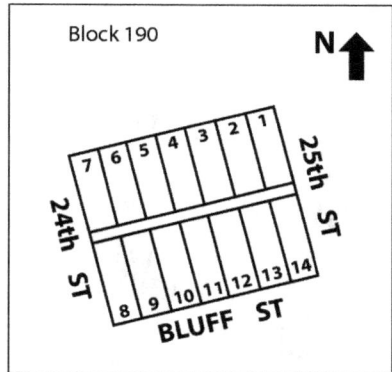

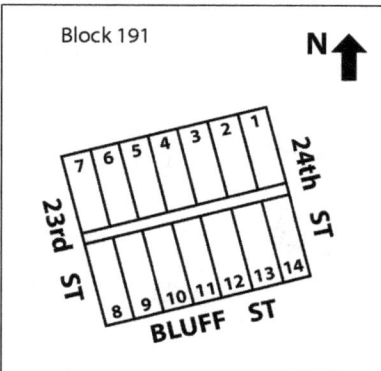

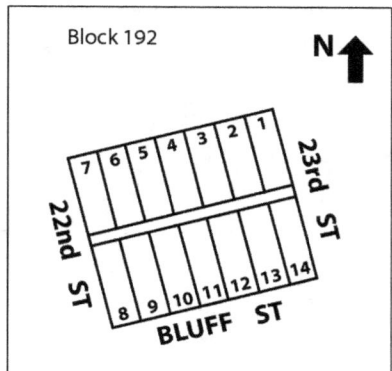

193–198

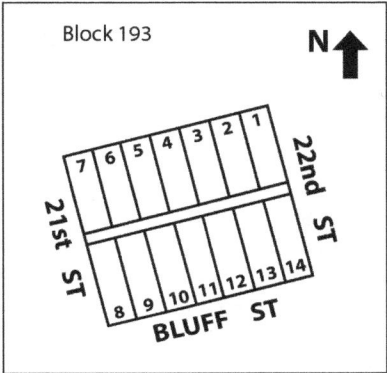

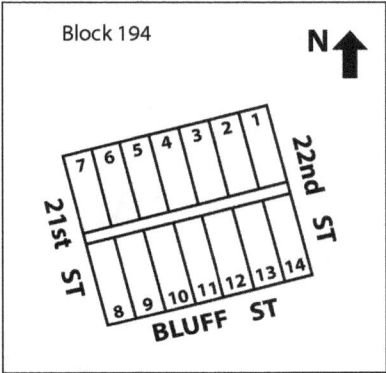

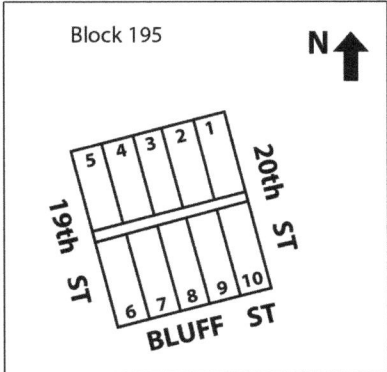

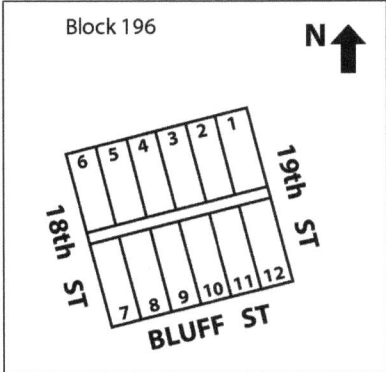

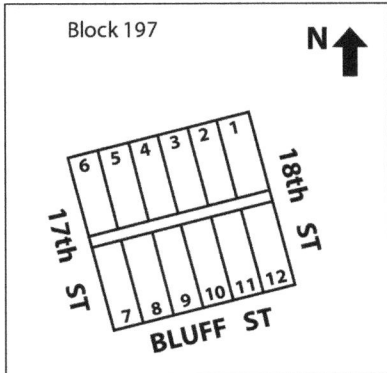

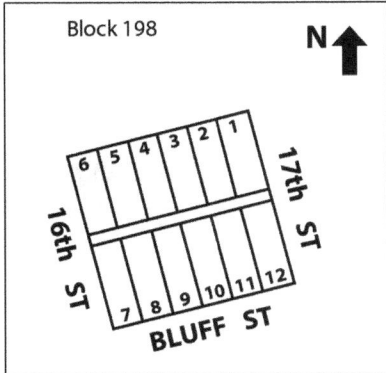

199–200

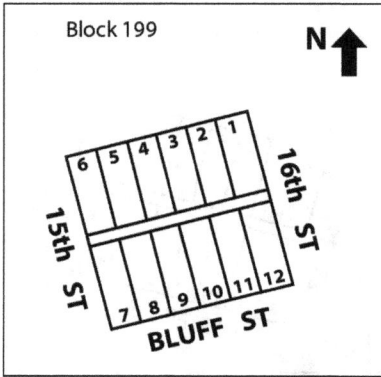
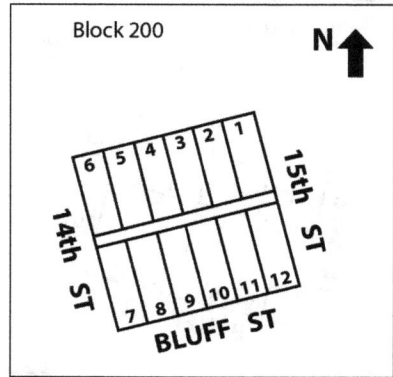

Index

F

Fay, Alvah 10, 26
Fray, J P 5
Fray, Patrick J 35

G

Gardner, C H 70, 74
Gardner, Chas 11
Gardner, Chas H 71
Gibbons, J V 69
Gillett, C B 81
Goodwin, Oliver P 25
Goodwin, O P 25, 34, 72
Goss 10, 21, 22, 23, 24, 25, 26, 28, 36,
    48, 84, 85, 86, 87, 88, 89
Goss, C J 10, 14, 47, 61, 77
Goss, J C 47
Goss, Pell & Co 87
Goss, Pell & Lowe 10, 14, 21, 22, 23, 24,
    25, 26, 28, 36, 48, 61, 84, 85, 86,
    87, 88, 89
Green, Henry 57
Greenly, J H 8, 11, 42, 76
Griffith, T A 73
Griggs, H O 60
Grovenor, A H 64

H

Hackelman, Geo 86, 87, 88, 89
Hackelman, George 27
Hackleman, George 6, 84, 85
Hall, John R 9, 27, 31, 39, 40
Hamilton 24, 29
Hamilton, T R 9, 27, 28, 39
Harris 70
Harris, A W 26, 27, 74, 81, 84, 85, 86,
    87, 88, 89
Harris, H B 55
Heath, Clark W 7, 11
Henderson 63
Henderson, E J 72
Henderson, J D 17, 39, 43

Henderson, Jno D 5
Hill, Sylvester 22, 71, 82, 86
Hobbie, Orman E 57
Holden 39
Hoole, Geo 25
Hoole, George 22, 48
Horse Sale 76, 77
Horsfal, David 26
Horsfall, David 10
Horton, George H 79
Horton, George W 26, 32, 78
Horton, G W 77, 78, 81
Hotchkiss 5, 30
Hotchkiss, S D 7, 25
Houley, H C 78
Housel, P M 77
Howard, W G 63
Howard, W S 63
Hughey, William K 55, 56
Hughey, Wm K 28
Hunt 84
Hunt, A M 27, 33, 40, 84, 85, 86, 88, 89
Hunt & Appleton 84
Huntington, Gilbert 53

I

Indian claim 61, 63
Irwin, Jno B P 53
Irwin, J P B 11, 49

J

Jacobs, A 56
Jameson & Jameson 35
Jamison, J H 76
Jamison, J M 86
Jamison, Joseph H 63
Jones, T J 9, 18, 19, 30, 31, 35, 42, 43,
    68, 69, 70, 84, 86
Jones, W W 29

Additional Colorado Research Titles

If you borrowed this copy from a library and would like to order a copy, please send a check or money order to: Iron Gate Publishing, P.O. Box 999, Niwot, CO 80544. Our books are available online to institutions through Lightning Source, to individuals at Amazon.com and on our website:

www.irongate.com

Boulder County, Colorado Probate Court Fee Book, 1874-1890: An Annotated Index
ISBN 978-1-879579-88-0 $11.95 + $4.00 S&H

Brainard's Hotel Register, Boulder, Colorado, 1880: An Annotated Index
ISBN 978-1-879579-86-6 $15.95 $5.00 S&H

Boulder County Commissioner's Journal, 1861-1871: An Annotated Transcription
ISBN 978-1-879579-77-4 $45.99 + $5.00 S&H

Boulder County Commissioners Journal, 1871-1874: An Annotated Transcription
ISBN 978-1-879579-91-0 $39.95 + $5.00 S&H

Brainard Hotel Register, 6 March-18 December 1880: An Annotated Index
ISBN 978-1-879579-86-6, $15.95 + $5.00

Colorado's Territorial Masons: An An'notated Index of the Proceedings of the Grand Lodge of Colorado, 1861–1876
ISBN 978-1-879579-85-9 $29.95 + $5.00 S&H

Boulder, Colorado Teachers, 1878-1900: An Annotated Index
ISBN 978-1-879579-93-4 $11.95 + $4.00 S&H

Boulder County, Colorado District Court Execution Docket, 1875-1885: An An'd Index
ISBN 978-1-879579-94-1 $11.95 + $4.00 S&H

Denver, Colorado Police Force Record, 1879-1903: An Annotated Index
ISBN 978-1-879579-81-1 $11.95 + $4.00 S&H

Boulder, Colorado Births 1892–1906: An Annotated Index
ISBN 978-1-879579-79-8 $11.95 + $4.00 S&H

Arapahoe County, Colorado Territory Criminal Court Index, 1862-1879: An An'd Index
ISBN 978-1-879579-70-5 $11.95 + $4.00 S&H

Boulder County Probate Court Appraisement Record A, 1875-1888: An Annotated Index
ISBN 978-1-879579-72-9 $11.95 + $4.00 S&H

Boulder County Assessor's Tax List, 1875: An Annotated Index
ISBN 978-1-879579-55-2 $11.95 + $4.00 S&H

Boulder County Assessor's Tax List, 1876: An Annotated Index
ISBN 978-1-879579-56-9 $11.95 + $4.00 S&H

Boulder Valley Presbyterian Church Records, 1863-1900: An Annotated Index
ISBN 978-1-879579-58-3 $11.95 + $4.00 S&H

Boulder's Masonic Pioneers, 1867-1886: Members of Columbia Lodge No. 14, Boulder County, Colorado Territory
ISBN 978-1-879579-57-6 $15.95 + $4.00 S&H

Publishing Titles

If you would like to order one of these books, please send a check or money order to: Iron Gate Publishing, P.O. Box 999, Niwot, CO 80544. Our books are available online to institutions through Lightning Source, to individuals at Amazon.com and on our website:

www.irongate.com

Set Yourself Up to Self-Publish: A Genealogist's Guide
    ISBN 978-1-879579-99-6 $19.95 + $5.00 S&H

Publish Your Genealogy: A Step-by-Step Guide for Preserving Your Research for the Next Generation
    ISBN 978-1-879579-62-0 $24.95 + $5.00 S&H

Publish Your Family History: A Step-by-Step Guide to Writing the Stories of Your Ancestors
    ISBN 978-1-879579-63-7 $24.95 + $5.00 S&H

Publish a Local History: A Step-by-Step Guide from Finding the Right Project to Finished Book
    ISBN 978-1-879579-64-4 $24.95 + $5.00 S&H

Publish a Memoir: A Step-by-Step Guide to Saving Your Memories for Future Generations
    ISBN 978-1-879579-65-1 $24.95 + $5.00 S&H

Publish a Biography: A Step-by-Step Guide to Capturing the Life and Times of an Ancestor or a Generation
    ISBN 978-1-879579-66-8 $24.95 + $5.00 S&H

Publish a Photo Book: A Step-by-Step Guide for Transforming Your Genealogical Research into a Stunning Family Heirloom
    ISBN 978-1-879579-67-5 $24.95 + $5.00 S&H

Publish a Source Index: A Step-by-Step Guide to Creating a Genealogically Useful Index, Abstract or Transcription
    ISBN 978-1-879579-68-2 $24.95 + $5.00 S&H

Publish Your Specialty: A Step-by-Step Guide for Imparting Your Research Expertise to Others
    ISBN 978-1-879579-76-7 $24.95 + $5.00 S&H

www.ingramcontent.com/pod-product-compliance
Lightning Source LLC
Chambersburg PA
CBHW052215270326
41931CB00011B/2356